ADVENTUROUS PUB WALKS
IN
WARWICKSHIRE

Roger Noyce

COUNTRYSIDE BOOKS
NEWBURY, BERKSHIRE

COUNTRYSIDE BOOKS
3 Catherine Road
Newbury, Berkshire

To view our complete range of books,
please visit us at
www.countrysidebooks.co.uk

ISBN 1 85306 837 3

Designed by Peter Davies, Nautilus Design
Maps by the author
Photographs by Margaret Noyce

Cover photograph supplied by Bill Meadows shows the
countryside around Ilmington

Produced through MRM Associates Ltd., Reading
Typeset by Mac Style Ltd, Scarborough, N. Yorkshire
Printed by Woolnough Bookbinding Ltd., Irthlingborough

CONTENTS

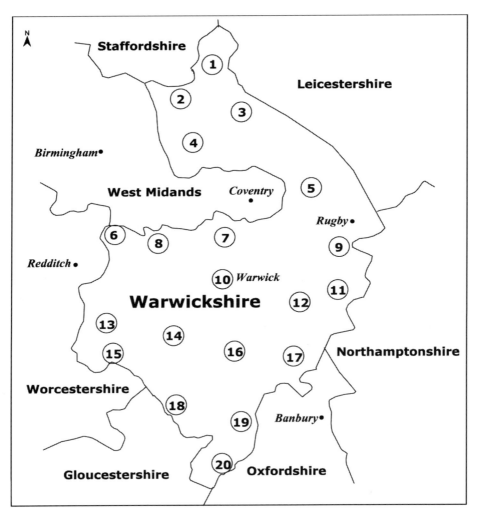

AREA MAP SHOWING THE LOCATION OF THE WALKS

INTRODUCTION

A walk in Warwickshire is an adventure into history for there are so many wonderful places of historical interest to visit. This is a most beautiful county where you can combine adventurous walking with an unsurpassed English history. There are many castles and large country houses scattered around and there are picturesque villages to wander through and historic English pubs to visit.

Colourful narrowboats making their way along a picturesque canal or up a flight of canal lock gates; attractive villages of honey-coloured local stone, with streets of thatched cottages; gentle hills inviting you to share their stunning views; a sparkling river as it meanders through rolling countryside; the reflections of sailing boats on a beautiful lake; walking through attractive woodland amid a carpet of bluebells; relaxing with a pint in the beer gardens of an old English pub; strolling along a footpath through fields of golden wheat; the visual impact created by a huge castle – these are just a few of my favourite things that can be enjoyed in abundance in the county of Warwickshire.

There are few serious hills in this fertile area set in the very heart of England. The walks are circular, based on good pubs serving good food, and they are certainly long enough and demanding enough to present a challenge, although you do not have to be super-fit to tackle them. I cannot offer you the muscle-straining, calf-killing slogs that can be found in some parts of the country, but in this seemingly unchanging rolling landscape there are adventures and enjoyments of a different kind to be had. Warwickshire is a county of attractive peaceful villages which can be reached on narrow lanes still relatively free of traffic.

This is Shakespeare country and the footprint of the famous bard appears almost everywhere. William Shakespeare (1564–1616) is probably the most famous author the world has seen, and he was born and brought up near the beautiful Warwickshire town of Stratford-upon-Avon, drawing upon his life's experience in an area that inspired the richness of his imagination. In his youth, Stratford was an important market town and this gave him the opportunity to note the manners, dress, and speech of the tradesmen, farmers, milkmaids, lawyers, and others who attended on market day. Boasting a population of 1,500 persons (London's was only 200,000 at that time), Stratford was then a centre of government and of rural business matters with one of the finest grammar schools in the country. Today, the swans gather by the Clopton Bridge in Stratford to be fed by the many tourists who come to pay homage to the Bard.

Evidence of the county's rich past is all around. The medieval county town of Warwick is dominated by its 14th-century castle, while nearby Kenilworth Castle was a stronghold for lords and kings of England in the 11th and 12th centuries. Ragley Hall is the home of the Marquess of Hertford; Coughton Court is the home of the Throckmorton family, and history connects it with the Gunpowder Plot; Baddesley Clinton Manor House contains a number of priest holes built by Nicholas Owen to hide priests from Cromwell's men; Packwood House has an amazing garden of yew trees; Upton House is a fine William and Mary mansion; Compton Wynyates is one of the most beautiful Tudor houses in the British Isles, and Charlecote House is where Shakespeare is said to have been caught poaching deer.

Adventure with me and visit these amazing places as you walk along some of the most attractive footpaths in the country, taking time to enjoy refreshments in one of the historic pubs in the wonderful county of Warwickshire. Most of the walks cross farmland at some point and so the usual countryside courtesies are important, such as closing gates behind you. The footpaths in Warwickshire are generally well marked and old wooden stiles are being replaced by metal kissing gates; you may find improvements have been made since I did the walks for this book.

The surface of the footpaths is generally good, so that older walkers and families with young children should have little difficulty. The weather in this country is well known to be unpredictable and so it is especially important to always have the right clothing. In dry weather, the paths will be firm underfoot and normal outdoor walking shoes should be adequate. In dry and hot weather always take a hat with you as protection against the sun; and a bottle of water is essential. In wet weather, or during the winter months, there could be moist stretches on some footpaths and then comfortable walking boots are vital, as is a set of waterproofs. If it is really cold, warm layers of thinner garments are better than one thick one, as they allow you to change according to the conditions during the walk.

There can be few greater pleasures in life than to combine a visit to a pub with a delightful country walk, and each walk includes a pub situated about halfway around the route. Some information is provided about the pub and the food and the drinks it can provide; the telephone number and e-mail address (where known) are also included to enable you to make further enquiries before your visit.

I am pleased to invite you to stroll along the lovely footpaths in the beautiful county of Warwickshire and to visit some of its fine pubs and inns. I wish you many happy adventures.

Roger Noyce

POLESWORTH AND THE ALVECOTE POOLS

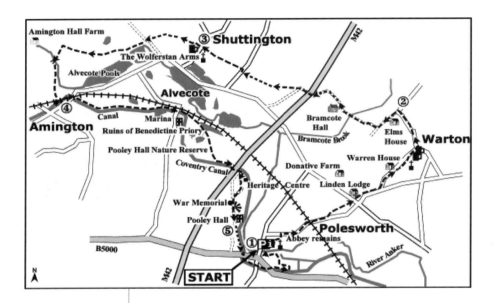

Distance:
9¹/₄ miles

Starting Point:
*Polesworth Hall
Court car park.
GR 262023*

Map: OS Explorer 232 Nuneaton and Tamworth

How to get there: *Polesworth is 28 miles north of
Warwick and 11 miles east of Sutton Coldfield. Leave the
M42 motorway at junction 10 and take the A5. In Dodon,
go left down Long Street and follow the signs into
Polesworth and Hall Court car park in Bridge Street.*

THE NUNNERY GATEWAY IN POLESWORTH

This pleasant walk in north Warwickshire enables you to experience a small part of monastic England and to see the beautiful abbey church and vicarage in Polesworth. From there, the walk takes you through typical rolling Warwickshire countryside to the villages of Warton and Shuttington; the fine old church in the attractive village of Shuttington is a little treasure.

The impact of the Industrial Revolution is never far away, but there is peace and tranquillity to enjoy with lovely farm tracks offering pleasant views over the Alvecote Pools. You may be lucky enough to see graceful herons coming in to land on the River Anker, and as you return along the towpath of the Coventry canal towards old Pooley Hall you will encounter the remains of an old Benedictine priory.

The Wolferstan Arms is a spacious old pub situated at the top of a hill overlooking Tamworth and the Alvecote Pools. This country inn offers a warm welcome and an extensive range of dishes on the main menu and specials board, and dining here is always a pleasure. Pub meals are also served in the no-smoking restaurant, where you can enjoy panoramic views. If you visit on Sundays you will have a choice of beef, lamb, or turkey roast, and there can be no better way to relax than to sit in the delightful beer garden with a pint of Marston Pedigree. Telephone: 01827 892238.

① Leave the car park at its rear and walk to the right of the library building; then bear left towards the abbey church. Spare time to view the old nunnery gateway.

Polesworth is the ancient town where Egbert, the first Saxon king of all England, built a nunnery, of which his daughter Editha was abbess. Today the abbey church (founded in 827) and the nearby nunnery gateway can still be seen. A 17th-century tithe barn and a few timber-framed houses also bear witness to the town's historic past.

Go along the fenced footpath to the left of the churchyard and at its end bear left into **High Street**, opposite to **Rofs Croft**. Head right up the street, passing by the primary school, and then cross over the railway bridge to leave the town.

About 250 yards beyond the railway bridge, bear left and climb the bank to go over a stile into a large cultivated field; then aim for a stile set to the right of **Linden Lodge**. Cross over the driveway, keeping to the right over a further stile; then walk to the right of the house's grounds to a stile, going over the entrance driveway to a small farm. The route bears right through a gateway by the road hedge and you walk along a fenced path off the road. This path leads round the edge of fenced pastureland where Shetland ponies run free.

At the end of the large field, go onto **Church Road** and head left towards **Warton** village. As you proceed up the quiet road, bear right into the recreation ground and leave this just before the churchyard. Continue past the church and two pubs – **the Hatters Arms** and **the Boot Inn** – to reach the main road through the village. Head left along the pavement, following the road signed 'Austrey 2' and sparing time to admire the many fine houses along the way. (2 miles)

② At the end of the village go left up the driveway past **Elms House** and head into open countryside. After about quarter of a mile along a mainly tarmac driveway, go right and walk half-right (north-west) towards **Bramcote Hall** (unfortunately the old building is in a poor state of repair). Continue past the building and the farm complex, walking along the good track that curves left; you begin to hear road noise as you near some trees by the busy M42 motorway.

Cross the motorway by the farm bridge and at the small copse follow the waymark direction over three fields: you will walk to the left of a field hedge to arrive at a lane. Go right along the lane for about 50 yards. Then go left over a stile and walk the clear footpath set to the left of the hedge, pausing from time to time to enjoy the fine view over **Alvecote Pools Nature Reserve** to your left. This footpath leads to the village of **Shuttington** by an attractive large house. The route bears right along the right-hand side of a private house. Go left past the entrance to the house and pass through the churchyard to emerge opposite to the **Wolferstan Arms** pub in the village. (2 miles)

The tiny Norman parish church of St Matthew was originally a chapel of nearby Alvecote Priory.

THE WOLFERSTAN ARMS, SHUTTINGTON.

When strolling through the churchyard, look out for the gravestone of the fattest man in 18th-century England – Thomas Spooner, who at 40 stone 9lbs was the century record breaker.

③ Cross over the road and continue to the right of the hedge by the village green into **Milner Drive**. As you bear left you will descend over a pair of stiles that lead you back into open countryside. The footpath crosses a couple of large fields with **Alvecote Pools Nature Reserve** to the left. The route arcs right around a standing of trees and then left to continue half left (SW). You can walk on the path to the right of the field edge, or you may venture to walk along the fisherman's path around the top of one of the pools. If you do this, bear right past fishing station 50 to return to the main footpath, where there is a choice of stiles. Go over the stile to the right and walk to the right of the wire fence. This takes you away from the pool and you turn left, following the waymarkers to a footbridge over the **River Anker**; about 200 yards to your right is the private **Amington Hall**, with its numerous farm buildings.

Cross the footbridge (you may perhaps see herons by the riverside) and follow the footpath across pastureland, with the river close on your left. A hand gate leads onto a stone path and a road over the railway line. Descend the far side of the bridge into **Amington**. Cross over the main street and bear right to descend to the **Coventry Canal** at **bridge 66**. (1³/₄ miles)

④ Head left along the canal towpath and follow it for about a mile. You will pass the backs of many attractive gardens, with the railway line down to your left. You are likely to see a number of narrowboats making their way along the canal and to your left you will pass a pool of bullrushes. Leave the canal at **Alvecote Bridge** (no. 59) to visit the remains of the Benedictine priory, which is set in trees.

Return to the towpath and now take the footpath into the nature reserve. This leads into the trees to the left of the towpath and you will pass various pools where wildfowl congregate. Keep to the main path through the reserve to emerge by the side of the towpath once again as you approach the **M42** motorway bridge. Proceed right over **bridge 56** and walk beneath the motorway bridge.

You have just walked through the area of former Pooley Hall Colliery, which was the first coalmine in the country to install pit-head baths and to generate its own electricity from surplus steam used to drive the winding gear.

Bear left past the **Pooley Field Heritage Centre**, which provides an insight into mining history, leaving the complex along its driveway to reach **Pooley Lane**. Head left along the lane past the war memorial, which commemorates the workers and owners of Pooley Hall Colliery who lost their lives during the First World War. There is a delightful view to your left overlooking the canal and with Donative Farm sitting proudly on the hill beyond. Continue along the lane; in the trees to your left you may catch a glimpse of **Pooley Hall**. (2 miles)

Set in the trees overlooking the River Anker, Pooley Hall was built in 1509 and is now a private residence. Both William Shakespeare and the poet Michael Drayton are purported to have been regular visitors to the hall and its vicarage.

⑤ Immediately after passing the driveway to the hall, go left through a gap in the hedge and walk along the footpath that goes down gently towards the canal. You will emerge by a tarmac footpath set to the left of some new houses and this will lead you to the B5000 road bridge. Descend to the towpath of the **Coventry Canal** and follow it until you reach **bridge 51**.

From here ascend into the village of **Polesworth**. Head northwards and stroll through the pleasant gardens up to the **River Anker**. Bear left and walk beside the river; then go right over the footbridge to reach a path junction. Head right and then left to return to the car park. (1¹/₂ miles)

Date walk completed:

KINGSBURY WATER PARK

BODYMOOR HEATH WATER IN KINGSBURY WATER PARK

Distance:
8 miles

Map: OS Explorer 232 Nuneaton and Tamworth

Starting Point:
*Kingsbury Water
Park visitor centre
car park.
GR 204959*

How to get there: *Kingsbury is 23 miles north of
Warwick and 13 miles north-east of Birmingham. Leave the
M42 at junction 9 and proceed along the A4097 towards
Kingsbury. Go left at the first road island towards Marston
and follow the clear signs into Kingsbury Water Park.*

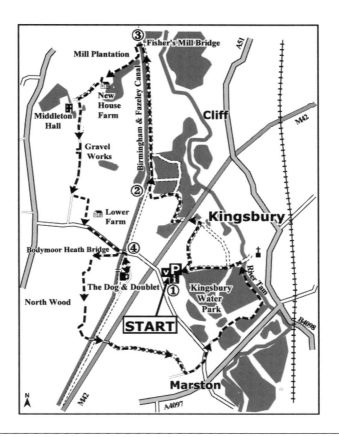

This easy walk starts from Kingsbury Water Park, where you can feed the ducks or watch the energetic partake of various water sports. The route takes you past several of the lovely lakes in the park and along the towpath of the Birmingham and Fazeley Canal. It then ventures into typical Warwickshire countryside, passing through attractive woodland to visit Middleton Hall. Although in the countryside, the industrial aspect of the Midlands area is never far away and you will pass through a gravel works. Soon, though, you are back by the canal for lunch at the Dog & Doublet, and as you return to the water wonderland you will pass attractive houses in Marston village.

The Dog & Doublet is a traditional country inn with heavily beamed ceilings and it retains plenty of 'olde worlde' charm. A doublet was a close-fitting garment worn by men between the 14th and 18th centuries, and it seems that versions of this garb were sometimes used to dress dogs, particularly those used by wild-fowlers. With his dog wearing a brightly coloured doublet, the sportsman was able to keep a keen eye on the animal as he sent it to retrieve a fallen bird. The original purpose of the building, erected in 1789, was to stable the horses pulling the many narrowboats up and down the adjacent Birmingham and Fazeley Canal. You can enjoy meals and drinks at your leisure in a paved beer garden alongside the canal and watch the abundant wildlife and brightly painted narrowboats pass by. Alternatively, if you are feeling energetic, you can stroll along the canal banks, taking in the scenic views and tranquil settings.

As you would expect, you can choose drinks from a wide variety of beers and ciders, including Bass and a range of guest ales. For the connoisseur, there is also a recently refreshed wine list containing wines you can enjoy with your meal or simply sup while watching the world go by. Website:www.dog-and-doublet.com; e-mail:info@dog-and-doublet.com; telephone: 01827 872374.

The Walk

① From the **Kingsbury Water Park visitor centre** go through the car park and bear left up a good tarmac path into woodland.

Sited near to the River Tame, the area occupied by Kingsbury Water Park was originally meadowland and riverside fields. In the 1930s it became a mineral extraction site, which was eventually transformed into a vibrant and thriving country park in the 1970s. Today it comprises 30 lakes and pools attracting some 220 species of wildfowl each year. Kingfishers and great crested grebes nest in the park, and otters have now returned to the River Tame. The West Midland Bird Club has been involved in advising on the development of bird habitats in the park for some years and has a permanent information centre overlooking Broomey Croft Pool.

Keep to the clear route up the left-hand edge of the park and after about three quarters of a mile you will arrive at a track (**the Heart of England Way**) coming in from the right. Go left here and pass beneath the **M42** motorway. Continue in your eastwards direction, following the waymarkers for the **Heart of England Way** as you progress through the water park. (1¹/₂ miles)

② Soon you will pass through a car park set to the right of a camping site, to arrive by the **Birmingham and Fazeley Canal**.

The Birmingham and Fazeley Canal, completed in 1789, was built by John Smeaton to form a link between the Oxford and the Trent and Mersey Canals. Until then London-bound goods from Birmingham had to travel a longer route along the River Severn. It took many years before the canal fulfilled its complete aim because certain areas became very congested. In 1844, the Tame Valley Canal and the Birmingham and Warwick Junction Canal were opened, and the Birmingham and Fazeley Canal became fully attractive to carriers. Sadly, canals have ceased to be used as a means of transporting goods around the country but in recent years they have become an important leisure facility. There can few more pleasing sights than watching a colourful narrowboat make its way up the canal past the Kingsbury Water Park.

THE DOG & DOUBLET, BODYMOOR HEATH

17

Bear left to enjoy the peaceful scene at **Curdworth Locks** and then retrace your steps to proceed up the canal towpath in a northerly direction for about a mile. The walking is easy along this straight stretch of the canal, where the peace is interrupted only by the chugging of the occasional canal boat or barge. (1 mile)

③ Leave the towpath (and the Heart of England Way) at **Fisher's Mill Bridge**. Cross the bridge and in about 100 yards turn left onto a footpath that proceeds along the side of the canal and then bends right along the left edge of **Mill Plantation**. It becomes a hedged/fenced footpath along the side of the woodland, and there is a stretch of water to your left. The plantation is a picture in spring when you will see bluebells, white wild garlic, and pink campion amid the trees. You pass to the right of **New House Farm** and soon arrive on a track that leads you towards **Middleton Hall**.

For over 700 years Middleton Hall has retained its original deep splayed window in the west wing of its main building. In the 15th century, timber-framed north and east wings were added. The hall was the home of the Willoughby family, and in 1711/12 Thomas Willoughby became the first Lord Middleton. In 1966, the entire estate was purchased by Amey Roadstone Corporation for sand and gravel extraction, and the hall became unoccupied. Following the efforts of conservationists, a trust was established in 1980 and the hall and some 40 acres of gardens have been restored. Adjacent to the hall are the Middleton Courtyard shops.

Head left before the hall buildings onto a wide stone track. In about 700 yards you will pass between the buildings of a gravel works; continue along its approach road. In a further 500 yards go left over a stile and walk along a signed footpath towards a gap in the hedge by an oak tree. Head right along the hedge-side footpath to a hand gate onto **Bodymoor Heath Lane**; then go left until you reach Bodymoor Heath Bridge over the **Birmingham and Fazeley Canal**. Descend to the towpath going beneath the bridge to reach the **Dog & Doublet** public house. (2 miles)

There are some pretty cottages with well-tended gardens beside the canal at Bodymoor Heath Bridge. Between Kingsbury and Bodymoor Heath there are about 11 locks which make up the Curdworth flight and lower / raise the water an amazing 76 feet 4 inches.

④ Retrace your steps to **Bodymoor Heath Bridge**. Cross over the bridge and then go left along a lane past houses to a fenced track. Go over the stile at the end of the track and head left along the edge of several cultivated fields. The route starts on the right of a small stream but later you cross over to walk to the left of the stream. A stile leads into a further field and you continue along the bank of the small stream for about 250 yards, with **North Wood** across the field on the far bank.

Bear left and cross over the field to **Marston Field** canal bridge among the trees to your left. Cross the canal and go over the footbridge across the M42 onto a farm track that descends gently into the village of **Marston**. You arrive in **Seeney Lane** and, passing **Home Farm** on the right, reach the **Old Kingsbury Road**. (2 miles)

⑤ Head left along the **Old Kingsbury Road** and pass a number of large attractive houses. At the end of the road, bear left along **Bodymoor Heath Lane** to a road junction. Here, cross the lane and bear right onto a quiet lane heading towards **Kingsbury Water Park**. In about 250 yards you will pass into the park through a gateway. Go straight ahead along the tarmac pathway, which runs in a generally north-easterly direction.

Soon you will join part of the **Centenary Way** and should follow its waymarkers until you arrive by **Hemlingford Bridge**.

The Centenary Way (see Walk 12) is one of two walking routes that pass through Kingsbury Water Park, the other being the Heart of England Way, a 100-mile route, which starts at Bourton on the Water in the Cotswolds and passes through the water park to reach Milford at the top of Cannock Chase.

Just before the bridge, turn left and walk along a delightful waterside footpath with the **River Tame** to the right and **Hemlingford Water** to the left. Ahead of you is Kingsbury's Norman church, which stands majestically over the water park.

Just before reaching another bridge over the **River Tame**, head left along a raised footbridge and head into the water park, following the waymarkers and going left along the route past **Bodymoor Heath Water**. Leave the **Heart of England Way** to continue ahead until you arrive back at the visitor centre. (1 1/2 miles)

Date walk completed:

HARTSHILL HAYES COUNTRY PARK AND THE BLUEBELL CARPET

WHITE HART INN, RIDGE LANE

Distance:
7^1/$_2$ miles

Starting Point:
Visitor Centre at
Hartshill Hayes
Country Park.
GR 316943

Map: OS Explorer 232 Nuneaton and Tamworth

How to get there: *Hartshill Hayes Country Park is 11
miles north of Coventry. Approach Hartshill on the A444
road and when near to Hartshill follow the clear signs to
the country park.*

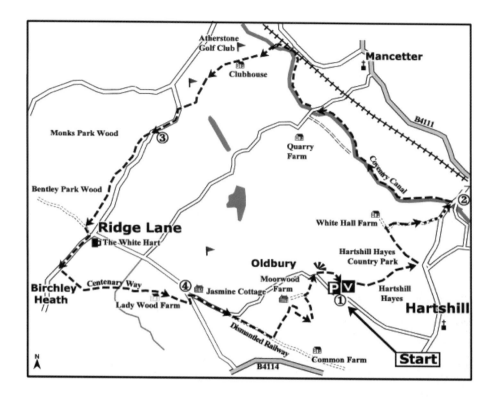

*T*his lovely walk in North Warwickshire starts from Hartshill Hayes Country Park and takes you through delightful woodland in the park on the way down to the Coventry Canal. The walk progresses through an undulating golf course and you can digress into beautiful woodland to walk a well-defined footpath which in spring offers a treat: a carpet of bluebells that is nothing less than magnificent.

Lunch is available at the *White Hart* in Ridge Lane, and then you progress through attractive countryside and farm complexes. Your return route passes a hilly area of gorse before you return to the country park to enjoy a fine view over the neighbouring county of Leicestershire. Complete your day perhaps with a cup of hot soup or a coffee at the visitor centre in the country park.

Tucked away in the small village of Ridge Lane is the 18th-century **White Hart** public house. Erected about 1835, the buildings were originally cottages, which were sited just down the lane from where Boudicca (a queen of the Britons) is reputed to have committed suicide following her defeat at the hands of the Romans.

The pleasant, carpeted lounge and bar feature an original lead range and the well-stocked bar can offer all the usual beers and lagers with cask ales – Bass Brew XII – and occasional guest beers too. A warm welcome will await you, together with good food and comfortable accommodation if you need it. The inn is open from 11 am to 11 pm throughout the week and from noon to 10.30 pm on Sundays. Food is available at any time during opening hours, and you can select from a choice of freshly prepared mouth-watering dishes of steaks, fish, chicken, or curry. In addition, there are daily specials to look out for; you are sure to find something to suit your taste. On a warm summer day the garden is a very pleasant place to eat. Website: www:travelpublishing.co.uk; telephone: 01827 712038.

The Walk

① From the visitor centre, walk to the left of the buildings, into the trees at the back, and along the footpath that goes to the right. If you keep to the main path, it will lead you down through the lovely woodland and in about half a mile you will cross over a footbridge and ascend towards the road in **Hartshill**. Do not go onto the road but go left along the footpath at the back of the houses.

Hartshill village stands on an island of ancient rock, a ridge which obscures from view the rows of miners' cottages and houses. Above Hartshill is a Quaker meeting house and a Quaker school dedicated to George Fox, the founder of the Society of Friends, who was born in the Leicestershire village of Fenny Drayton. Michael Drayton the poet was born in the village in Chapel Cottage in 1563. He was a friend of William Shakespeare and sang of the River Anker in his 'Polyolbion', describing it as 'trifling betwixt her banks so slow'. He died in 1631 and was buried in Westminster but is well remembered in Hartshill. He is commemorated in a bus shelter which was built in the shape of a scroll, from local stone that was donated by the nearby quarry owners. Sir John Betjeman dedicated the memorial and quoted from Michael Drayton's poem 'A Fine Day':

A PATH IN HARTSHILL HAYES COUNTRY PARK

*'Clear had the day been from
   the dawn
All chequered was the sky
Thin clouds like scarfs of
   cobweb lawn
Veiled heaven's most glorious
   eye.'*

The path is undulating, and you will pass through an area of bushes to arrive in the valley. With **White Hall Farm** up to your left, turn right and go over the stile onto a farm track. Keep to the track, which will join Woodland Lane at the edge of **Hartshill** village. Turn left and walk down the road, crossing the bridge over the **Coventry Canal**. (1¹/₂ miles)

The Coventry Canal, completed in 1790, passes below Hartshill. James Brindley was originally contracted to build it but he was sacked from the project because all of the authorised capital had been spent. In spite of its early financial problems, the canal, which provided an important link between Coventry and the Trent and Mersey Canal, proved very profitable. In its heyday it was a cheap means of transporting coal from the Bedworth coalfield; today it is part of a huge network of leisure canals operating throughout Warwickshire and the West Midlands.

② Bear right into a small car parking area and then turn right under the canal bridge and walk along the towpath. Take this easy pathway for the next 1¹/₂ miles or so. After passing beneath **bridge 37**, leave the canal towpath at **bridge 38**.

Cross over the bridge and take the clear wide track, with **Atherstone Golf Course** to your right. Continue up this track, soon passing in front of the club house to walk up a footpath going along the edge of the golf course. After about half a mile of delightful scenery, climb over the stile onto a lane that passes in front of buildings to reach a road. Head left along the side of the road for about 500 yards. You will have **Monks Park Wood** to your right and a pleasing view over the undulating countryside to your left. (2¹/₂ miles)

③ Go right onto the footpath that heads into the woodland, taking the left fork so that you are walking just inside the trees, more or less parallel with the road. Follow the well-defined path for about three quarters of a mile. This is delightful walking, and in spring you will be treated to a stunning carpet of bluebells. Soon you will arrive at a good track and here you turn left to reach the road in the hamlet of **Ridge Lane**; the **White Hart** pub stands on the corner opposite. Head right along the road towards **Birchley Heath** until you reach the end of the woodland (now called **Bentley Park Wood**).

Just before you reach the first house in **Birchley Heath**, turn left down a track to a stile and then continue along the left-hand side of the field hedge. This will take you past a lovely spinney where in spring you will find more bluebells. Continue along the clearly marked footpath of the **Centenary Way** (see Walk 12). Cross over the two footbridges at the field end and bear right towards **Lady Wood Farm**. The footpath generally goes to the left of the main buildings, but you can walk through part of the farm complex to the right of the large barn. Continue ahead along the left-hand edge of the next field and then bear left over a stile to reach another stile set to the left of a row of cottages. Go over this onto the road and head left to a road junction. (2¼ miles)

④ Turn right along the lane towards **Oldbury**, passing **Jasmine Cottage** and some attractive woodland on your left. Where the road bends sharp left, go straight ahead, still following the waymarkers of the **Centenary Way**. You will walk along a wide, hedged track (a dismantled railway line), which begins to narrow as you progress.

Just after going over a stile by the second fence, with the buildings of **Common Farm** in the valley to your right, turn left and descend onto a footpath going generally in a north-easterly direction, with **Moorwood Farm** visible ahead. You are still on the **Centenary Way**, but there has

been a small diversion here. Walk the clear, well-used path that arcs right, away from **Moorwood Farm**. In about 250 yards, go left along a clear permissive footpath and then bear left again. You will walk past gorse bushes and the pond of the farm as you continue to curve left. The path becomes a track; at its end go right along another farm track. As you approach the end of the track go left over a stile and walk to the left of the field hedge up a bank. Now bear left towards a stile set in the far left corner of the field and cross it onto the road. Cross the road and go to a bridleway gate to enter **Hartshill Hayes Country Park**, where you will be welcomed by a magnificent view over the nearby countryside.

Hartshill Hayes Country Park is set on the very top of the ridge above the village, and on a clear day forty churches can be counted from this vantage point. The park is popular with local people, being a delightful mix of woodland and open space.

Bear right along the top of the ridge and make your way back to the visitor centre. (1¼ miles)

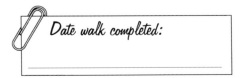
Date walk completed:

SHUSTOKE RESERVOIR WALK

SHUSTOKE RESERVOIR

Distance:
10 miles

Starting Point:
The Severn Trent car park in Shustoke. GR 225910

Maps: **OS Explorer 221 Coventry and Warwick, OS Explorer 232 Nuneaton and Tamworth**

How to get there: *Shustoke is 12 miles east of Birmingham. It is best approached on the M42 motorway. Leave the motorway at junction 7a and take the A446 into Coleshill. Cross over High Street in Coleshill and follow the road signs to Shustoke. The car park is on the left as you enter the village.*

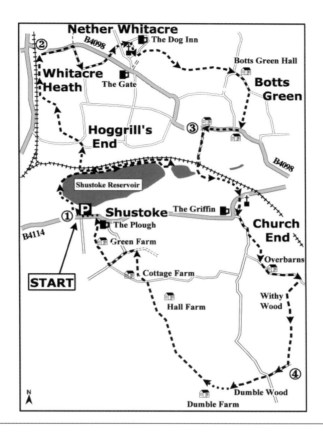

This easy walk takes you around beautiful Shustoke Reservoir and into the nearby countryside, passing by several good public houses along the route. After a short stroll alongside part of the main reservoir, you walk along stretches of the Heart of England Way and progress towards the village of Nether Whitacre. Farm fields lead you past the magnificent black and white building of Botts Green Hall, and then the Heart of England Way takes you past historic St Cuthbert's church in the old part of Shustoke. The old rectory will catch your eye as you go through Church End, and there are pleasing views to enjoy before you head southwards to Dumble Wood (known locally as The Dell), which is carpeted with bluebells in springtime.

The Griffin occupies a 17th-century timber-framed building, which has a brick exterior and is situated on a sharp bend in the attractive village of Shustoke. Inside you can experience the delights of an old country inn, for it is full of oak timbers – with lots of 'bits' hanging from the ceiling – and has a slightly sloping floor. The ceiling beams are lined with beer mats from down the years. This pub is well worth a visit just to sample the real ales (Marston's Pedigree, Theakston's Old Peculier, Highgate mild, and Charles Wells' Bombadier), and you will enjoy traditional pub food, which can be eaten in the beer garden. Until a few years ago Church End Brewery, situated in an old coffin workshop behind the Griffin, brewed a range of cask-conditioned beers. A visit to the Griffin Inn is an experience that will enrich your life and uplift your soul. Telephone: 01675 481205.

 *The Walk*

① From the **Severn Trent car park** bear left past the public toilets then join the 'circular walk' and walk clockwise around the larger of the two reservoirs. This is a delightful walk, embracing a panoramic view over the main reservoir, with the **church of St Cuthbert** on the skyline.

Shustoke Reservoir together with neighbouring Whitacre Water Works serves Coventry and Nuneaton. At weekends the reservoir is an engaging scene, with the local sailing club providing entertainment for visitors, and fishermen attempting to catch trout from its banks.

To your left lie a stream and the railway line, with rolling Warwickshire countryside beyond. When you reach the central strip of land, go right and then left over a footbridge and ascend steps to the smaller upper reservoir. Bear left over the bridge crossing the stream to a junction of paths by the fence near the railway line. Head left along the clear, hedged path by the side of the railway line, following the **Heart of England Way** for about half a mile. Just before a bridge go right, crossing the rail track and climbing the field on the other side.

In about 300 yards cross a lane; then go through the gate opposite, to walk across the next field, aiming for a stile in the opposite corner. Now turn right to cross a large field and go left over a couple of footbridges. Then turn right and walk by the side of the railway line for 500 yards, passing residential houses in **Whitacre Heath**. (3 miles)

② Turn right and walk up **Middle Lane** for about 350 yards; then turn right down **Bakehouse Lane**. At the road junction go left along **Deep Lane**; then cross over **Gate Lane** and the **B4098** to arrive in **Nether Whitacre**. Look out for the approach to the church and turn right onto this clear footpath, passing the church to reach a lane.

Take time to wander through the unassuming village of Nether Whitacre. Whitacre Hall, a private residence about a mile away from the village, was once the home of the Jennens family, who were early ironmasters of Birmingham. The village church is of recent origin but has an old tower with interesting stone grotesques; there are four odd little faces on one side, all in a row!

Cross over the lane and go over the stile by a gate to a large house. At the end of the property, turn left and cross pastureland to a footbridge. Proceed over the footbridge and cross over cultivated fields, following the clear waymarkers to reach a lane junction.

Here, bear left and walk along the quiet lane signed to **Botts**

THE GRIFFIN INN, SHUSTOKE

Green. This will take you in front of **Botts Green Hall**, with its crisp black-and-white exterior dating back to 1593.

A drawing of Botts Green Hall can be seen on www.ewgreen.org.uk. The drawing was completed in 1926 by William Albert Green (Will A. Green), who concentrated on historic buildings in the English Midland counties.

Where the lane bends to the left, continue ahead through a farm gate and walk along field paths to reach the **B4098**. Turn right and walk beside the quiet road for about 500 yards. (2¼ miles)

③ Now turn left down a hedge-lined track that leads you back to the railway line. Cross over the line and go through the hand gate into the grounds of **Shustoke Reservoir**, following the **Heart of England** waymarkers past the gates to the reservoirs. At the junction of paths turn left, going through a wooded area and over stiles; soon you will be circling the edge of a farm field. The path arcs round to the right and up to the **B4114**. Here go left, keeping to the roadside for about 15 yards; then cross it and go through a kissing gate. Passing through pastureland by **St Cuthbert's church**, go up to a tarmac path/road that leads past the church and up to **Shawbury Lane**.

Shustoke is very much a rural village, with a large area of the land belonging to Sir William Dugdale of Blyth Hall. The village's most famous resident was Sir William Dugdale, the author of The Antiquities of Warwickshire, first published in 1656.

Up until 1650, the village surrounded the church of St Cuthbert, but after the plague hit the people moved to its western end, which forms the nucleus of the village of today. The church was struck by lightning in 1886 and was damaged in the resulting fire; it was repaired in 1887 and still marks the eastern extremity of the village. Nearby are five almshouses which were originally part of the village school. They are now administered by the Huntbach Trust.

Head left along **Shawbury Lane**, passing the very attractive old rectory and soon cross a stile to cross a cultivated field, following here the waymarkers towards a gap in the hedge to the left of a building. Then cross the next field to rejoin **Shawbury Lane**. Head left along the lane, past cottages named '**Overbarns**', and continue along the road; you will have a clear view of the huge complex of **Daw Mill Colliery** in the valley to your left.

Just after a sharp right-hand bend in the road, go right at a waymarker post and into open countryside. The path bends right and then left, and continues to the left of **Withy Wood**, which offers a spectacular carpet of bluebells in spring. After passing the end of the wood, the path continues southwards by the side of the field hedge. Initially you walk to the left of the hedge, then pass to the right of it, and finally back to the left before crossing a stile to a lane. (2$^1/_4$ miles)

④ Turn right into the lane and continue to a junction; go straight across and follow the clearly waymarked footpath across a footbridge into **Dumble Wood**. The even path wends its way through a truly delightful stretch of woodland, with a stream to the right. Follow the waymarkers for the **Heart of England Way** until the path goes to the right over a stile and into the trees. Here you continue ahead along the side of the woodland, and soon **Dumble Farm** will be to your left.

At the end of the trees the path curves to the right and you go over a

footbridge into the next field. Continue by following the waymarker direction for the path that proceeds half left (north-west) over several fields, crossing the fields to the left of **Hall Farm** to reach a lane. Cross over the lane and continue along the footpath opposite, passing to the right of **Cottage Farm** to arrive on a driveway which turns left to reach a lane called **Hollyland**. Head left up the lane.

Just before **Ash Cottage**, turn right over a stile and follow the footpath over a cultivated field, aiming for a stile set to the left of **Green Farm**. Cross this and continue to a further stile, which is set to the right of **Greenacre** (a cottage) and leads into **Back Lane**. From here you emerge at the green in **Shustoke**, close to **the Plough** public house. Make your way to the **Coleshill road (B4114),** where you go left and then right to arrive back in the **Severn Trent car park**. (2$^1/_2$ miles)

<table>
<tr><td>*Date walk completed:*</td></tr>
</table>

HARBOROUGH MAGNA AND THE GHOST OF BRINKLOW

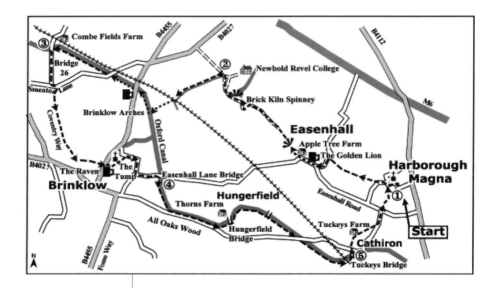

Distance:
9 miles

Map: OS Explorer 222 Rugby and Daventry

Starting Point:
All Saints' church in Harborough Magna.
GR 477793

How to get there: *Harborough Magna is 4¹/₂ miles north of Rugby. From Rugby take the B4112, which passes through Harborough Magna. Go left into the main street and park with consideration by the side of the road.*

THE OXFORD CANAL NEAR HUNGERFIELD

*T*his excursion into North Warwickshire starts from the peaceful village of Harborough Magna, passing through Easenhall before progressing into open countryside. Here you pass by the fine buildings of Newbold Reve College and walk beneath Brinklow Arches to reach the Oxford Canal. A pleasant stretch along the towpath takes you past the colourful premises of Rose Narrowboats and Stretton Wharf on the way to Grimes Bridge. Picturesque scenery remains with you as you continue into the small town of Brinklow for refreshments at the Raven. The route then goes past The Tump, where for over a century Lang's Ghost has cast its spell, before returning to the towpath and the colourful array of narrowboats. From there a walk through delightful countryside brings you back to Harborough Magna.

In 1865 a serving girl at the **Raven Inn** named Sarah Haynes was found strangled on Brinklow Hill (The Tump). Suspicion fell on a self-proclaimed Satanist named John Lang and an occult society that met in the grounds of nearby Coombe Abbey. Sometime later Lang himself disappeared and both Sarah's and his disappearance remain unsolved. For over a century Lang's ghost was said to haunt both Brinklow Hill and the Raven Inn, which stands just below it. The ghost of a dark Victorian figure is said to have been seen in the bar, with frightening poltergeist activity being reported by landlords and customers alike. The jukebox would turn itself on in the middle of the night, even when it was not plugged in, and the beer pipes in the cellar would fly around as if moved by unseen hands. On one occasion, a porcelain figurine on the shelf behind the bar lifted into the air and flew across the room, in full view of over a dozen dumbfounded customers.

Today the Raven is a friendly family pub, which is open every day between noon and 11 pm (Sunday to 10.30 pm). There is a choice of Banks's Bitter, Marston Pedigree, and a guest real ale to quench your thirst. Lunch is available between noon and 2 pm (3 pm on Sunday), and from 6 pm to 8 pm in the evening you can select a 'sizzler' to eat in the bar area or in the pleasant garden. Telephone: 01788 832655.

 *The Walk*

The peaceful village of Harborough Magna, recorded in Domesday Book as Herdeberge, lies in unspoilt countryside near to Rugby and adjoins Harborough Parva. It has a pleasing mix of private residences, a smithy dating from the 17th century, and a pub, the Old Red Lion, dating from 18th century. All Saints' church, which dates from the 14th century, is perhaps the village's main feature. Set in its Victorian west tower is an unusual clock-face picturing at the quarters the four beasts (the four Evangelists; Revelations 4:6-8).

① From **All Saints' church** walk towards the edge of the village. A few paces after passing **Holly Cottage**, turn right over a stile and walk along a footpath across cultivated fields towards the village of **Easenhall**. To reach the village, go over a footbridge near to an attractive thatched cottage, **Campbell's Cottage**. Go left to a road junction by the village green, with the old **Congregational chapel** (now the village hall) facing you. Note the attractive American style house called **Brooklands**.

The tiny village of Easenhall consists of about 40 houses but boasts a fine pub, the Golden Lion, which is a popular local refreshment place. The village has no post office, no shop, no school, and no church, but the residents own the small, one-room Congregational chapel, which is now used as a village hall.

If you are out walking the lanes of Easenhall at night, look out for the phantom horseman! He is said to be the ghost of One-handed Boughton, who died at Old Lawford Hall. Attempts were made to exorcise his ghost by placing his remains in a phial, which was thrown into the village pond, but the ghost story is still part of local legend.

Head right along **Main Street**, passing the **Golden Lion pub**. Where **Main Street** bends left to become **Brinklow Road**, bear right and proceed along **Farm Lane**. You will pass an impressive house on the left and at its rear is the village cricket pitch. Continue up the lane past **Apple Tree Farm**. Go left through the bridle gate and then bear right through a farm gate, walking along the bridleway set to the right of a wire fence. At the brow of the hill there is a superb view ahead that embraces the imposing buildings of **Newbold**

THE RAVEN, BRINKLOW

Revel College, rebuilt in 1716 and now used as a teacher training establishment. Go through the hand gate and walk along a green track that leads to the right, past trees, to a pair of footbridges on the perimeter of **Brick Kiln Spinney**. Here go left and then right to join a farm track through the trees. At the end of the spinney, bear left and stroll past the lakes of the college, walking along the driveway, where there is a good view of the front of the building. Do not go through the gate across the drive but bear left to continue along the bridleway and reach the main entrance drive to the college. (2 miles)

② Turn left and go along the footpath set to the right of a stream. In about three quarters of a mile you pass beneath a railway bridge to arrive at the **Brinklow Arches**. Proceed through the tunnel under the **Oxford Canal**; then go right and climb the steep steps to arrive by the canal. Head left along the towpath, past **Rose Narrowboats**, where you can visit the gift shop, and **Stretton Wharf**, and continue to **Grimes Bridge** (no. 26). (1³/₄ mile)

③ Leave the towpath, and go past a well-maintained cottage to reach the road junction with **Smeaton Lane**. Go left along **Smeaton Lane** and at the first corner go right onto a good footpath, crossing over an interesting old footbridge. Now follow the

waymarkers of the **Coventry Way** into the small town of **Brinklow**. The path hugs the left edge of several fields and then bends left to reach the edge of the village. After passing the town's recreation area, you arrive in **Barr Lane** and will emerge in **Broad Street**, almost opposite **the Raven**.

Brinklow's 13th-century church is an interesting place to visit while you are in the village. See if you can spot the fascinating headstone of Thomas Bolton, the deaf and dumb woodcutter. The headstone shows a bundle of faggots, a woodman's glove, an axe, and a gorse bush. He was felling trees during the reign of George III but never heard a sound or uttered a word. His epitaph reads as follows:

> *He chiefly got his livelihood*
> *By faggoting and felling wood,*
> *Till Death, the conqueror of all,*
> *Gave the feller himself a fall.*

Walk up **Town Yard** (to the left of **the Raven**) onto a footpath that leads to a stile. Ascend the steep steps opposite to arrive back in open countryside with **The Tump** immediately ahead of you. Take the clear path to the left of **The Tump** to reach **Ella Lane**.

The Tump is an ancient mound which is believed to be a burial ground dating back to pre-Roman times. A stroll up to the top of the mound offers a good view over Brinklow village.

Head right along the lane, which bends to the right, to arrive at a junction with **Easenhall Lane**. Here, turn left and in about 300 yards you will reach **Easenhall Lane Bridge** (no. 34) over the **Oxford Canal**. (1³/₄ miles)

④ Descend to the right of the bridge and turn right along the towpath of the **Oxford Canal** for the next 2 miles. After about 500 yards of pleasant towpath walking, you will pass moored narrowboats and a small car parking area, where visitors feed the ducks. Continue along the towpath, with **Cathiron Lane** and **All Oaks Wood** to your right and the canal to your left, as it weaves its way through **Hungerfield** and into **Cathiron**. Pass **Cathiron Farm** (on the far bank) and proceed to bridge 43 (**Tuckey's Bridge**). (2¹/₂ miles)

The Oxford Canal, started by James Brindley, was one of the earliest winding contour canals in southern England. Sadly, when

Brindley died in 1772, the advent of the railway was having an adverse effect on its commercial potential and the canal, being incomplete, was inefficient for carrying goods. It was Samuel Simcock who eventually completed the canal route to Oxford in 1790. It then proved to be one of the most profitable canals and held off the competition of the railways right through until the 20th century.

⑤ Go onto **Cathiron Lane**; go left to a junction, and then go left again. In 160 yards, go right, cross a stile into a field, and walk along the footpath going northwards towards **Tuckey's Farm**. Cross over the stile to the right of the farm and continue over the next field, passing a lonely midfield stile and taking care to avoid any wet patches. With **Lodge Farm** to your left, leave the field by a stile onto **Easenhall Road**. Go right along the road, past a row of houses, and then, when opposite the junction with **Cathiron Lane**, go left over a stile and take the hedged footpath that arcs left to arrive back in **Main Street, Harborough Magna** and **All Saints' church**. (1 mile)

Date walk completed:

EARLSWOOD LAKES BLUEBELL WALK

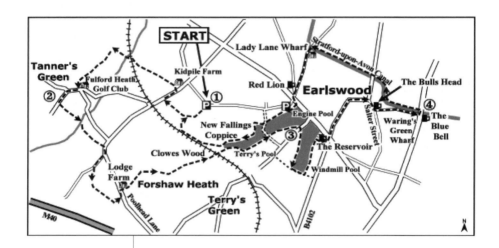

Distance:
9 miles

Starting Point:
Car park on the edge of New Fallings Coppice, off Wood Lane. GR 101743

Map: OS Explorer 220 Birmingham, Walsall, Solihull, and Redditch

How to get there: *Earlswood is 10 miles south of Birmingham and is best approached on the A3400 Stratford Road. From Shirley, go right along the B4102 road into Earlswood. Just before reaching the reservoir, go right into Valley Road, and then left into Wood Lane to reach the car park.*

CANAL REFLECTIONS NEAR WARING'S GREEN WHARF

*T*his walk is ideal in spring when carpets of woodland bluebells adorn your way. Starting in a majestic coppice, it proceeds over delightful open countryside, crosses a golf course, wanders over typical rolling Warwickshire farmland, and dallies along ancient leafy lanes. After passing Forshaw Heath you walk along the banks of bubbling Spring Brook and pass glistening silver birches in Clowes Wood Nature Reserve before crossing the railway line and circumnavigating the pools of Earlswood Lakes, where wildfowl can be seen at play. After refreshments at the Reservoir you pass more inviting country pubs on the way to the Stratford-upon-Avon Canal and then return to the lakes along the opposite bank. After one final bluebell wood, you arrive back at the car parking area.

Around 1900, Earlswood became a popular tourist centre for the working people of Birmingham. The **Reservoir Hotel** was then advertised as 'An Ideal Resort for Pleasure Seekers', and bank holidays were busy and profitable times. However, drunken revellers brought havoc to the peaceful rural community. A resident of the time described the scene on one bank holiday: 'One young lady was so far gone with drink that she took off all her clothes and danced naked, much to the amusement of the crowd. However she was quickly covered and arrested.' Little appears to have changed!

Although still a place for people to enjoy themselves, the recently refurbished Reservoir public house is now a Millers pub, offering the newest brand in Scottish and Newcastle Retail family dining. It is a regular haunt for walkers in the area, and you will be made very welcome. Bread is baked on the premises each day and fresh fish dishes are available from the extensive menu. (You can even place your order through computers on the tables.) A great chef and an Impinger oven (no microwave on the premises) ensure that the food is excellent. Children can enjoy the freedom of the large garden and there are free refills of coke, diet coke and lemonade. Telephone: 01564 702220.

The Walk

① From the car park enter the coppice and walk along the footpath, following the small waymarker posts through the bluebell wood. Cross the footbridge and bear right, finally leaving the woodland to cross over arable land to a hedged path. This leads to the road, with **Earlswood station** 150 yards to the left. Turn right up the road for about 200 yards.

Just before reaching **Kidpie Farm**, turn left through a gap in the hedge and walk along a footpath by the field hedge, proceeding half left (north-west) for the next half mile. The path starts on the left of the hedge then enters trees (more bluebells) before continuing to the right of the hedge. Another field is crossed before the path descends beneath the railway bridge.

Maintain your direction and climb a hedged pathway (this can be a bit muddy after rain, but it too is lined with bluebells in spring); to the left is **Fulford Heath Golf Club**.

In about 150 yards, go left over a stile and walk along the clearly marked footpath through the grounds of the golf course – a lovely stretch of open walking, but take care not to interfere with the golf.

After walking by the greens you pass near the club house and arrive at the road in **Tanners Green**. Turn right towards **Wythall** at the junction and stroll along the quiet road for about 125 yards past some large houses. (2 miles)

② At the junction go left down **Barkers Lane** and in about 250 yards turn left again, along a footpath signed to **Forshaw Heath**. This takes you along the back of houses and through shrubs and trees. Then cross over a large cultivated field on a well-defined headland which takes you to **Forshaw Heath Lane**.

Turn right at the lane and right again at the road junction. Then, in another 300 yards, bear left into **Juggins Lane**. After a further 300 yards, go left through **Graves Coppice**, keeping to the right-hand edge of the trees and then bearing right beyond the prefabricated homes. Cross over the next field and go left at a stile to arrive in **Poolhead Lane**. Go left along the lane for about 100 yards.

Go right over the stile set to the right of **Lodge Farm** and follow the footpath past the farmhouse. Go over the stile to the left of the farm gate and follow the waymarker directions to a footbridge in the far

THE RESERVOIR, EARLSWOOD

corner of pastureland. Cross over the footbridge over the stream and recross by a second footbridge. Head left, keeping to the right of the field hedge. Soon you will be walking to the right of **Clowes Wood**, where there is an abundance of bluebells and other wildflowers. Follow the waymarker direction and in about half a mile you will cross over the railway line onto a delightful path by the side of **Terry's Pool**; you have arrived by the first of the **Earlswood Lakes**.

Three pools form Earlswood Lakes (Engine, Windmill and Terry pools) offering a total of 85 acres of feeder water for the Stratford-upon-Avon Canal. When they were constructed in 1821 they were interlinked by ditches and controlled by sluice gates to allow water to be moved from one lake to another. Using the pumps in the engine house, water would then be transferred into the feeder canal from Engine Pool. In 1936 the original engine, which had operated for 110 years, was removed, and the pumps were then worked by electricity.

Today the lakes have become a leisure facility for local people and day trippers from Birmingham, offering opportunities for walking, fishing, and sailing, enhanced by the added attraction of the Earlswood Lakes Craft Centre.
Stroll along the lakeside path for the

next three quarters of a mile, as far as the thin stretch of land that separates **Engine Pool**; you can stroll onto this to enjoy a wider view of the lakes. Continue along the right-hand bank of **Engine Pool** and soon you will reach a roadway that bisects the lakes. (2^1/$_2$ miles)

③ Cross the road and proceed through the hand gate opposite, bearing right to skirt **Windmill Pool**. Continue along the right bank and in about 400 yards turn right up a clear footpath that leads into the car park of the **Reservoir** public house.
  Leave the car park and bear left in front of the main building; cross over at the road junction and walk along the pavement of the **B4102**. Where the road bends sharp left, go right down **Salter Street**, passing by **the Bulls Head** public house and then turning left along **Lime Kiln Lane**. Pass **Waring Green Wharf** to reach **Warings Green Road**; the **Blue Bell Cider House** is opposite. (1^3/$_4$ miles)

④ Turn left to cross the canal bridge and then descend to the towpath of the **Stratford-upon-Avon Canal**,

The Stratford-upon-Avon Canal was built to ensure that the commercial interests of Stratford-upon-Avon were not overlooked when the canal system was set up at the end of the 18th century. The section from King's Norton to the Warwick

and Birmingham Canal was opened in 1803 and started a most prosperous period with canal traffic exceeding 180,000 tons at its peak – some 50,000 tons of coal were transported to Stratford-upon-Avon.

The Great Western Railway brought about the demise of the canal by purchasing it in 1845. By 1890 the tonnage carried had reduced to a quarter of that carried at its peak, and by 1950 only an occasional working boat passed along the canal. It quickly fell into disrepair but was rescued by the National Trust, which obtained a lease from the British Transport Commission and set about restoring the canal. This was completed in 1964 after four years of hard work by canal enthusiasts, assisted by prison labourers. Today the canal is a popular leisure facility for walkers and narrowboat enthusiasts.

Turn right under **bridge 19** and proceed along the towpath for the next mile, passing a large colourful selection of narrow boats moored in

Warings Green Wharf opposite. Pass beneath **bridges 17** and **18**, continue to **Lady Lane Wharf** (opposite is the base of the **Earlswood Motor Yacht Club**, which you can visit for a drink and food if you wish) and leave the towpath at bridge 16.

Ascend to **Lady Lane** and head left towards **Earlswood**. In about 500 yards you will pass the **Red Lion pub** and reach a road junction. Here, bear left into **Valley Road** and you will see **Engine Pool** on the right. A final right turn allows you to go through the hand gate onto the footpath and then continue along the right-hand side of the pool. You will soon be walking past the stretch of land that divides **Engine** and **Terry Pools** and you should continue along the side of **Terry Pool**. At its end, turn right up a path into the trees of **New Fallings Coppice** and a final dose of spring bluebells. The path lies beside the railway line until you join the outgoing footpath; go right here and retrace your steps to the car park. (2³/₄ miles)

Date walk completed:

KENILWORTH CASTLE AND THE TIPPERARY TRAIL

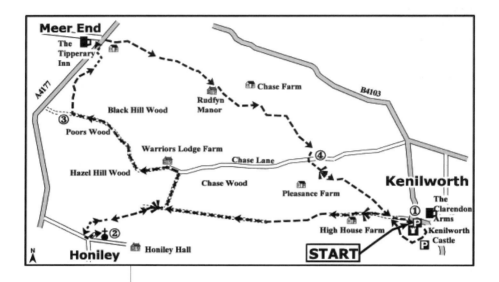

Distance:
8 miles

Starting Point:
Castle Green car park.
GR 279723

Map: OS Explorer 221 Coventry and Warwick

How to get there: *Kenilworth is just over 6 miles north of Warwick. Approach on the A46, turning left onto the A452 to Kenilworth. Go through the town, following the castle signs, and park in the parking area at Castle Green.*

KENILWORTH CASTLE

*O*n this adventure into English history you will have an opportunity to visit imposing Kenilworth Castle, which is now under the protection of English Heritage, and to see the fine baroque-style church of St John the Baptist in Honiley; you will encounter superb bluebell woods, and you will discover that, from Kenilworth, it's not a long way to Tipperary!

The walk starts by the famous castle, and good tracks take you into typical undulating Warwickshire countryside. From the beautiful landmark church at Honiley, still following well-established tracks, the route passes through enchanting mixed woodland and goes on to Meer End – and a chance to visit the pub associated with the famous song – before returning to the pleasant Warwickshire countryside. The superb half-timbered Rudfyn Manor will catch your eye, and you will enjoy an exceptionally fine view of the castle on your return to Kenilworth.

Most of the folklore that surrounds the **Tipperary Inn** relates to the pub's name. Despite the apparent Irish connection, the pub was named in honour of local man Harry Williams, who was, in part, responsible for the famous song 'It's a Long Way to Tipperary'. The actual composer was a man named Jack Judge and he wrote the song in 1912. In their early years the two men were neighbours, and Harry Williams kept a small country pub in Oldbury, called the Malt Shovel. Harry often lent Jack money, and Jack promised in return that if he ever wrote a best-selling song he would put Harry's name on it also. He kept his promise and both men made a small fortune from the royalties of the song, which became such a favourite during the First World War.

A visit to the inn is an enjoyable experience, and you will be assured of a warm welcome, good food, and good beer. Bass Bitter, Courage Directors Bitter, Everards Dry Hop Conditioned Tiger Best Bitter, and Tetleys Cask are the real ales on tap, and the food menu varies from home-made specials to à la carte offerings. Food is served from Monday to Thursday from midday to 2.30 pm and from 6 pm to 9 pm and on Friday and Saturday between midday and 2.30 pm and from 6 pm to 9.30 pm. Sunday lunch is available from midday to 2.30 pm.

If you call for an evening special, you might choose to indulge in Ardennes pâté served with warm toast, followed by grilled chicken breast in a chasseur sauce, with new potatoes and vegetables, and finally chocolate junkyard.

Website: www.tipperary.co.uk; email: info@tipperary.co.uk; telephone: 01676 533224.

 *The Walk*

① From the castle car park go through the hand gate situated to the left of the castle and stroll around the castle. You will go over the main entrance drive and can continue round the building to emerge in open land on its west side. Walk past the thatched pink cottage and go over a stile onto a track. Head left down the track, and after about 800 yards you will pass to the right of **High House Farm**, but do take time to look back and enjoy a fine view of the castle. Beyond the farm continue along the hedged footpath until you emerge in a large field of mounds called **The Pleasance**. Leave the field via a stile and maintain your generally easterly direction, now walking to the left of the field hedge. You will soon be walking on a wide green track with **Chase Wood** up to your right.

At the junction of farm tracks go ahead to the end of the next field, go over the stile and across the footbridge near the top of the field, and then take the footpath to the right of the field hedge, going over two further stiles to reach a country road. Turn left and go along the quiet road for about 70 yards; then turn left again, passing **The Malthouse**, to arrive at **Honiley church**. (2½ miles)

The first church on this site was founded by Simon de Montford when Honiley was 'an exempt peculiar'. St John's Well was a place of pilgrimage and 'St John's Bath and Our Lady's Bath were used respectively for the cleaning of incontinent penitents'. Sadly, the well is no longer accessible. St John the Baptist church in Honiley was built in 1723, and it is believed that Sir Christopher Wren drew up the design for the church when dining with John Sanders. Francis Smith, who came to Warwick to rebuild the town following the great fire of 1694, is believed to have been the builder. He was twice Mayor of Warwick before his death. The church certainly has a superb baroque-style west tower topped by an octagonal spire with a ball and

THE TIPPERARY, MEER END

weathercock on the apex. There are six bells in the tower, although the sixth (the treble) was only added in 1977, in celebration of the Jubilee of Queen Elizabeth II. The gate piers leading into the churchyard were carved with the elephant heads motif which is the insignia of John Sanders, who lived in nearby Honiley House. The elephant motif is repeated on the front pew in this very lovely church.

② When you have had your fill of the church, retrace your steps to the junction of farm tracks and then go left up the track to the left of **Chase Wood** (in spring this is a sea of bluebells).

At the top of the track turn left along **Chase Lane** towards **Warriors Lodge Farm**. Walk along the fenced path to the left of the barn and continue until just before reaching a gateway; here you bear right and follow another track, set to the right of **Hazel Hill Wood**. In about 300 yards the track bends left to separate **Black Hill** and **Hazel Hill Woods**. This very wide, open track may be a little muddy in wet weather, but it is a delight to walk. After some 600 yards of easy walking you will emerge from the trees to find yourself in the West Midlands. **Poors Wood** to your left is full of lovely larch trees. Look out for a stile to your right. (2¹/₄ miles)

③ Go over the stile and continue along a clearly marked public footpath towards residential properties. The path soon runs parallel with the **A4177**, passing a number of attractive houses; it may be a little muddy in very wet weather. After about half a mile the footpath bends left to reach the road. Cross the busy road, with care, and turn right along the pavement to the **Tipperary Inn**.

From the inn cross the **A4177** again and go down the farm drive opposite, passing several cottages and going over a stile into a field. Follow the clear waymarker that leads down the side of a farm cottage and into the open, walking in a generally easterly direction. A series of stiles take you back into Warwickshire, where the footpath bends gently to the right (south-easterly). Initially you walk to the left of the hedge; the path then switches to the right of the field hedge and after passing to the left of **Rudfyn Manor**, an attractive half-timbered building, it bends right and joins the **Millennium Way** heading towards **Kenilworth Castle**. Beyond the manor the footpath becomes a good wide green track; at a right bend you then walk to the right of the field hedge. The route passes through a couple of small copses and bends right to reach **Chase Lane** next to a pair of red brick cottages. (2¹/₂ miles)

④ Cross over the lane and go through the new metal kissing gate opposite. Follow the direction of the waymarkers, at first walking over pastureland; you will probably be able to see the top of **Kenilworth Castle** on the horizon. For the next ³/₄ mile continue along the well-used footpath, going in a south-easterly direction. You will go through further kissing gates as you progress over cultivated fields and soon you will reach a final gate that takes you onto the track, with the castle ahead of you.

The red sandstone towers, keep, and walls of Kenilworth Castle glow brightly in the morning and evening sun, imparting a mystical appearance to one of England's oldest castles, which has been the home to some of the most influential people in English history. Here you can experience a fascinating journey into the past and an age of grandeur and glory. You can stroll through the Tudor pleasure gardens and explore the fine rooms where kings and queens were once entertained. William Shakespeare, then just 11 years old, witnessed a lavish visit of Elizabeth I in 1575; 20 years later he wrote A Midsummer Night's Dream, *which, according to experts, bears strong evidence of his visit.*

The castle has links with Henry V, King John, Edward II and John of Gaunt. Perhaps you will agree that tales of this great fortress castle were enhanced in Sir Walter Scott's Kenilworth, *written in 1821.*

Go left along the track and bear right by the Pink Cottage. Now go left up by the castle wall to return to the car park. (³/₄ mile)

Date walk completed:

BADDESLEY CLINTON MANOR AND PACKWOOD HOUSE

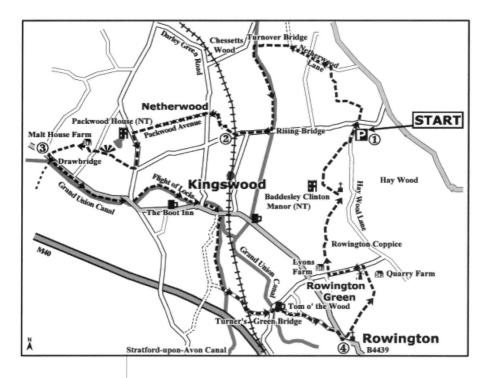

Distance:
10¹/₂ miles

Starting Point:
Hay Wood Lane.
GR 204723

Maps: OS Explorer 220 Birmingham, OS Explorer 221 Coventry and Warwick

How to get there: *Kingswood is 8 miles north-west of Warwick. Leave Warwick on the A429 and join the A4177 near the road island by the A46 junction. Bear left at Five Ways onto the A4141. Go left in Baddesley Clinton along Rising Lane, and then left again into Hay Wood Lane. Park with consideration.*

THE LAKE BEHIND PACKWOOD HOUSE

*T*his beautiful, easy circuit embraces two famous National Trust houses in the northern part of Warwickshire, as well as the spectacular Lapworth flight of locks on the Grand Union Canal.

The walk passes through pleasant open countryside to the canal, on a route dotted with picturesque cottages and prosperous farms. It passes the pointed gables, mullioned windows, and massive chimneystacks of Packwood House, with a chance to see the lake at the back of the building, before joining another arm of the canal, which eventually links with the Stratford-upon-Avon Canal at Kingswood. Along the towpath of the Stratford-upon-Avon Canal towpath you will experience crossing a remarkable split bridge before arriving in Rowington village. Lovely countryside and attractive woodland lead to Baddesley church and to the spectacular medieval moated manor house of Baddesley Clinton. Fine bluebell woods take you back to Hay Wood Lane.

The Boot Inn in Old Warwick Road, Lapworth is a tremendously popular country pub, set in the delightful, winding roads of Warwickshire and within easy reach of the Grand Union Canal. You are sure of a warm welcome and a delicious meal at the inn, for it has an outstanding local reputation and a great cellar stocked with cask ales and wines from around the world. The *Birmingham Post* has described the menu as 'very appealing ... full of tantalizing flavours, fresh ideas, novel taste combinations and a real sense of quality'; it will make your mouth water. The food varies from simple bubble and squeak to superb à la carte meals. If you have time, try my favourite: chicken liver parfait, apple chutney and warm brioche, followed by calves' liver, fondant potato, lime, tomato, and thyme sauce, perhaps with a side order of honey roast roots. Who needs a sweet?

Opening hours are from 11 am to 3 pm and 5.30 pm to 11 pm during the week and between noon and 11 pm at the weekend. Food is available from noon to 2.30 pm and from 6.30 pm to 9.30 pm.

Website: www.thebootatlapworth.co.uk; telephone: 01564 782464.

① Go up **Hay Wood Lane** to the junction with **Rising Lane**; here turn right and then left up a driveway to a former convent, passing its stable block. Leave the complex through a gate and go left over a stile onto a footpath that leads into attractive countryside. Initially you walk along a hedged path and then arc right, going along the back of houses to arrive in **Netherwood Lane** on a footpath set to the left of a large house. Head left along the lane, continuing ahead at the crossroads. In about 300 yards, bear left over a stile onto a hedged track going generally in a westerly direction. The track becomes a footpath, set to the left of a field hedge and bearing left to cross a smart gated footbridge. Continue along a farm track to **Turnover Bridge** and the **Grand Union Canal**.

The unique Grand Union Canal comprises eight canals built to link London with Birmingham, Leicester and Nottingham. Until 1920 the canals were owned and operated by separate companies and then, in 1929, they were consolidated to become one of the most important canal networks in the country. The Kingswood section joined the Stratford-upon-Avon Canal.

Turn left and follow the canal towpath to **Rising Bridge**. Having passed under the bridge, leave the towpath and crossing over the bridge go left along a country lane past attractive houses (2^1/$_2$ miles)

② Immediately after going over a railway bridge, turn right along a driveway past **Grove Cottage**. At the entrance gate to **Terets Farm**, bear right through a kissing gate and walk along the footpath by the laurel hedge enclosing the farmhouse garden to emerge onto a lane. Head right along the lane past **Uplands Farm** and then continue by going diagonally left up a farm drive to reach **Darley Green Road**. Go right for just 10 yards, and then cross the road and enter **Packwood**

Avenue over a stile. Follow the wide green track along its south-westerly course by a delightful avenue of beech and young oak trees. In about 750 yards go over a couple of stiles by a small lake and eventually you will reach a metal kissing gate that leads onto the road outside **Packwood House**.

Owned by the National Trust, Packwood House is an impressive timber-framed building dating back to the Tudor period. It has winding walks and terraces, but its most renowned feature is probably its topiary. Perfectly trimmed yew trees present a tableau of the

THE BOOT INN, LAPWORTH

Sermon on the Mount. The Evangelists are represented by trees that stand 30 feet high, and at the top is the Lord surrounded by a multitude of smaller trees.

Head left up the approach road to the house, pausing from time to time to enjoy the famous topiary garden to your right and in 325 yards you reach a junction. Turn right and then right again over a stile near the junction corner, walking to the right of some pretty cottages on a signed path that leads into open land. At the second stile you will enter the **Packwood estate** again. Continue around the field edge to a further stile and cross into the parkland; from here you can enjoy a superb view of the rear of **Packwood House** and its lake. Follow the waymarkers, go over the stile at the end of the parkland and cross the lane onto the driveway of **Malt House Farm**. Just before the impressive farm gates, bear left and cross a stile, heading left across pastureland to a final stile onto the **B4439**. (2¹/₄ miles)

③ Go left along the grass verge of the **B4439** for about 70 yards; then cross the road, entering a narrow farm lane that leads to **Drawbridge Farm**. In 50 yards you reach the **Stratford-upon-Avon Canal** at the drawbridge. Go left along the towpath of the canal, which flanks the road. Cross over the canal at

bridge **30** and return to the left bank at **bridge 32** for the descent past the **Lapworth** flight of locks.

The Lapworth flight of locks comprises 13 lock gates, nine of which are close together and present an impressive spectacle when negotiated by narrowboats.

Cross over **bridge 33** near the small canal shop; the **Boot Inn** can be reached from here. Continue along the towpath, on the right bank now, and after passing by several further lock gates and bridges you reach a junction with the **Stratford-upon-Avon Canal**. Go along the towpath of the **Stratford-upon-Avon Canal** towards **Stratford** and continue until you reach **Turner's Green Bridge**, where you cross over the road near to the **Tom o' the Wood** pub. Go over the stile to the right of the pub and ascend the field to **Mill Lane, Rowington** where you turn right to get to the **B4439**. At the **B4439**, turn right once again and walk along the pavement to **Rowington church**. (3¹/₄ miles)

Rowington village has important links with Shakespeare and among the winding lanes and the tall trees you may find Shakespeare Hall, a timber-framed house, where between 1574 and 1614 no fewer than four William Shakespeares lived. One of these Shakespeares was Thomas, whose son John was apprenticed to William Jaggard, the publisher. In 1623, his press produced an early collection of the Bard's comedies, histories and tragedies.

④ Cross over the **B4439** and go through the lychgate. Then, bearing left, leave the churchyard at the back of the church and pick up the **Heart of England Way**. You pass by **Quarry Farm** and a most attractive windmill conversion before passing through a gate onto a lane. Here, go left and walk along the lane for some 450 yards.

Now, go right through a gate to the right of **Lyons Farm** and walk the clear track which passes to the left of **Rowington Coppice**. The track curves gradually right until you reach a kissing gate near **Baddesley Clinton church**. Follow the path to the left of the church (the area near the church is ablaze with yellow daffodils in early spring) and you will soon emerge by **Baddesley Clinton Manor**.

You will cross a 200-year-old bridge over a wide moat to reach Baddesley Clinton Manor House, now in the hands of the National Trust. This gracious building, with its venerable walls and an embattled gatehouse with mullioned windows, timber gables and tall brick chimneys, dates from the 15th century. During the 16th century, when it was occupied by the Ferrers family, it became known as a safe haven for Catholic priests at a time of Catholic persecution. No fewer than three priest holes were built into the structure and no doubt saved a number of Catholic lives during this terrible period of English history.

Continue past the entrance gate and bear right, following the **Heart of England Way** and passing through a gate to walk to the right of a copse. Cross over the footbridge at the copse end and then go between some houses and over several stiles to arrive on **Hay Wood Lane**. Turn left along the lane to return to your car. (2^1/$_2$ miles)

Date walk completed:

DUNCHURCH AND DRAYCOTE WATER

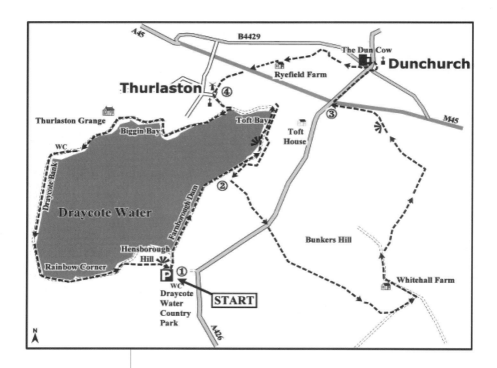

Distance:
9¹/₂ miles

Starting Point:
*Pay-and-display
car park at
Draycote Water.
GR 462692*

Map: OS Explorer 222 Rugby and Daventry

How to get there: *Draycote Water Park is 5 miles south-west of Rugby, just off the A426.*

THE SAIL-LESS WINDMILL IN THURLASTON

*A*fter an easy walk around beautiful Draycote Water Park, the route passes into nearby countryside and on to the village of Dunchurch, where there are thatched cottages to admire. In Thurlaston you walk close to a windmill with no sails and can wander around the peaceful picturesque village with its lovely houses and cottages. Back on the banks of Draycote Water there is a good tarmac lane that circles the lake, affording a chance to see the many waterbirds that frequent the park. In the summer, colourful sailing boats add to the picture postcard scene, and fishermen enjoy the freedom of the lake.

57

The Dun Cow dates back to 1560. Its heyday was in the 18th century, when it was a coaching inn on the London road and could stable some 40 pairs of horses. The name of this popular inn comes from a medieval romance. A cow that used to provide milk to the local villages became a monster that terrorised the villagers – perhaps the original 'mad cow'? According to the tale, the beast was defeated by the legendary Guy of Warwick.

Guests to the inn have included the Duke of Wellington, Louis XVIII of France, Princess (later Queen) Victoria, and the poet Longfellow, who is said to have written his smithy poem whilst staying at the Dun Cow. Bass and Tetleys real ales are on tap from 11 am to 11pm during the week and on Sunday between midday and 10.30 pm. Food is available between 12 noon and 10 pm during the week (9.30 pm on Sundays). Telephone: 01288 810305.

 *The Walk*

① Enter the country park, bearing right along a tarmac lane to the fishing lodge by the side of **Draycote Water**. When you approach the reservoir, bear right and stroll along the lane that circles Draycote Water's 240 hectares of nature reserve, passing initially along the top of **Farnborough Dam** wall. Pause before **Toft Bay** to enjoy a pleasant view ahead that embraces the fine church at **Thurlaston** and its sail-less windmill. At the end of **Toft Bay**, leave the reservoir by going right through a hand gate onto a footpath.

Go right over the stile onto the waymarked footpath that leads into trees on your right and pass a number of small pools; the path bends left and then right. Soon you are walking along a path just outside **Draycote Water Country Park**, which you follow until you reach a footbridge and a stile. (2 miles)

② Turn left into pastureland, walking by the side of a small stream and crossing a couple of fields to arrive at a stile onto the **A426**. Cross over the road, go through the gap in the hedge opposite, and continue in a generally south-easterly direction, walking to the right of the field hedge. At the next stile the path crosses the corner of a large field with a sizeable lake and with earth workings to your right. Keep to the left edge of the field and soon pass a further stile. As you continue you will go left over a small footbridge and then bear right over a larger one to return to the right-hand bank of a wider stream, now walking along a farm track. Bear left over a farm bridge made of railway sleepers on metal girders, to reach a junction with another farm track.

Head left along the track towards **Whitehall Farm**. Bear right past the farm, walking along its main drive. The drive bends left near to trees on **Bunkers Hill**, but you bear to the right (north-north-east) onto a waymarked path. This starts as a good green track with a pheasant wood to the right. After going over a stile into pastureland it becomes more of a footpath, and you continue to the right of the field hedge over several fields. Soon you are walking on a hedged track, at the end of which you go left onto a wide green path along the left-hand side of the field hedge. This path ascends by the hedge, giving a good view towards **Draycote Water** and **Hensborough Hill**, and then bends to the left. Here you walk near to the **M45** motorway to arrive at the **A426** on the outskirts of the village of **Dunchurch**. (3¼ miles)

③ Turn right and go along the pavement of the **A426** into **Dunchurch**, crossing the road bridge over the M45 motorway and passing by a number of attractive thatched properties, to find the **Dun Cow** at the crossroads in the middle of the village. The village square and **St Peter's church** are to the right of the crossroads.

THE DUN COW, DUNCHURCH

For centuries, Dunchurch has been a popular stopping place for travellers on the main London to Ireland route. It was a major coaching stop during the 18th century, when up to 40 coaches a day came here, and it appears that every property in the centre of the village was at some time an inn or ale house.

On 5th November 1605, the Gunpowder Plot conspirators met at the Old Red Lion Inn to await the news of Guy Fawkes' success in blowing up the Houses of Parliament. The Old Red Lion Inn still exists but is now a private residence known as Guy Fawkes House.

The 14th-century church of St Peter is mentioned in Domesday Book and is well known for its fine Norman doorway and font. It has a curious monument of folding doors to Thomas Newcombe, who was a 17th-century printer to three kings. He founded the fine almshouses, which have retained their 'olde worlde' appearance.

Today, Dunchurch is a quiet village in a designated conservation area. Thatched cottages mix happily with modern buildings, and there are charming 16th, 17th and 18th-century houses to be seen. Two elm-shaded greens, a maypole, stocks, and the steps of an ancient cross take you back in time. At the cross roads is a statue, created by

Joseph Durham, of Lord John Scott, who died while testing a vessel designed to overcome the problems of deep sea fishing.

Return to the crossroads. Cross over the busy **A4429** and then head right, past the **Dunchurch and Thurlaston Working Men's Club**. Turn left along **School Street**, passing a number of thatched properties and the infant school, and go down to the **Dunchurch Scout Group hall**. Here, turn right, and then left up a footpath set to the right of the playing fields, walking along the hedged footpath going to the right of **Ryefield Farm**. Continue ahead over pastureland, passing beneath the **M45** road bridge before diagonally crossing a farm field to a pair of stiles at the entrance to **Thurlaston**. Spare time to wander around this delightful village. (1¼ miles)

Domesday Book records its name as Torlauestone, and documentary evidence confirms that a church known as St Edmund's was licensed as early as 1360.

The present St Edmund's church was completed in 1848 on a site donated by local landowner Lord John Scott, with £1,000 raised by subscription and with a grant from central funds. It was used as a church on Sunday, with school lessons taking place there during the week. A flat was built into the tower to accommodate the schoolmaster and is still used today as private accommodation (the rope to the bell turret passes through one of its rooms).

④ Go through the farm gate to the left of **St Edmund's church** and follow the concrete driveway. Go over a stile into woodland and follow waymarks to re-enter **Draycote Water Country Park** through a hand gate. Now turn right and follow the contour of the lake round **Biggin Bay**. There may be a mass of coots or a few ducks on the water and the odd swan or an imperious heron may be feeding close to the water's edge. Occasionally a cormorant takes advantage of the 2,000 fish that are put into the reservoir each week by wardens. You are likely to see fishermen wading into the water or out on boats trying to catch their dinner in one of Britain's premier trout fisheries. To your right **Thurlaston Grange** can be seen, and you pass a golf course. At the end of the reservoir you pass a water treatment works and to your right you will see the spire of **Bourton-on-Dunsmore church**, about a mile away, with **Bourton Hall** to its right.

Bourton Hall is a large 18th-century stone mansion. It was built around 1790 on the site of an earlier house. After 1947 it was occupied by Jesuits for a period, and also used as a boys' preparatory school. It was then in danger of falling into disrepair but was purchased in 1979 by Ingersoll Engineers, who restored it to its former glory.

After going round the part of the lake known as **Rainbow Corner**, you approach the sailing club area; just before this (soon after passing by a picnic area), bear right up a footpath that leads to **Hensborough Hill**. Here you can enjoy a fine view of the surrounding area before passing the trig point (358 ft above sea level) and descending towards the park entrance and the car park. (3 miles)

Date walk completed:

HISTORIC WARWICK AND THE HATTON FLIGHT OF LOCKS

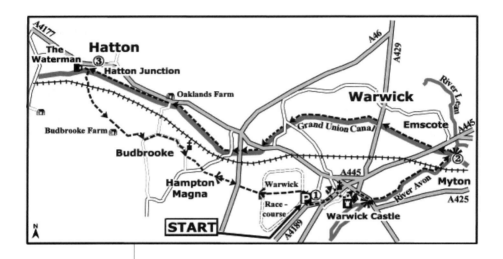

Distance:
9 miles

Starting Point:
Warwick
Racecourse car
park. GR 276674

Map: OS Explorer 221 Coventry and Warwick

How to get there: *Warwick is 22 miles south-east of Birmingham. It is best approached on the M40 motorway; leave at junction 15 and drive towards the town along the A429 Stratford road. As you approach the High Street, go left into Bowling Green Street and then left again into Friars Street (the A4189). The entrance to Warwick Racecourse is on the right, in about 150 yards.*

WARWICK CASTLE

*T*his is an easy walk around the wonderful county town of Warwick, offering an opportunity to visit the UK's finest castle (according to Channel Five). The route takes you through the historic town and along the banks of the River Avon and the towpath of the Grand Union Canal. You pass Hatton Locks, where you are likely to see colourful narrowboats making their way down the impressive flight of locks, and then cross gentle rolling countryside to the village of Budbrooke, which was the home of the Warwickshire Regiment for many years. Here you will see the gravestones of a number of the courageous soldiers who helped to protect us from our enemies during two world wars. A superb view over Warwick unfolds as you cross part of Warwick Racecourse at the end of a very pleasant walk.

The Waterman, with its position overlooking lock gates on the Grand Union Canal, is a delightful pub to visit. To sit in the gardens in the summer watching boats make their way along the canal, with a pint of draught Bass, Tetley, or Marston Pedigree in hand is a treat indeed. The pub is open all day from 11 am to 11 pm during the week (noon to 10.30 pm on Sunday). The restaurant offers a popular range of home-made food (which can also be eaten outside) between noon and 2 pm (2.30 pm on Saturday and Sunday) and, if you ring first, during the afternoon until 6.30 pm. Well behaved children and dogs are welcome. Telephone: 01926 492427.

 *The Walk*

① Leave the racecourse car park and go into **Friars Street** in Warwick.

Warwick is at the heart of Shakespeare country. Even though it was virtually destroyed by fire in 1694, the town rose again to provide a treat for the modern-day visitor, with so much historic interest crowded into such a small space. Spare time to wander round the lovely old town.

At the top of **Friars Street**, go right, and then head left into **High Street**. You will pass by the **Lord Leycester Hospital**.

This arresting group of buildings is dominated by the ancient chantry chapel of St James, which was built over the west gate into Warwick by Thomas Beauchamp, 12th Earl of Warwick, in the latter half of the 14th century and is adjoined by a superb half-timbered building. If you can spare time, you should make a point of also visiting the fine medieval hospital, the guildhall, and the county's own armoured regiment, which all nestle in this vicinity.

The Guild of St George was created under licence from Richard II in 1383. Thomas Beauchamp granted the benefice of the chantry chapel to the guild on its formation, and a range of rooms was built including reception, meeting and dining halls. In 1546 the guilds were dispersed by Henry VIII, the property of the United Guilds being saved from seizure through the admirable foresight of the master, Thomas Oken. In 1571, Robert Dudley, Earl of Leicester acquired the buildings and founded, under charter from Elizabeth I, a hospital for aged or disabled soldiers and their wives. In 1950, the guildhall was cleared, and the number of brethren temporarily reduced. In 1956 the hospital was restored and was re-opened by the late Queen Mother in 1966.

In a few yards bear left and walk along the pavement of **Brook Street**, crossing over into **New Street**. At its end, bear right to reach **St Mary's church**. (From the top of the tower there is a clear view of the town and the castle.) Go down **Church Street** back to High Street and cross over with care; continue up **Castle Street** opposite to arrive by **Warwick Castle**.

Warwick Castle, built on the site of a motte and bailey, was enlarged on the orders of William the Conqueror. The present structure dates mainly from the 14th and 15th centuries, the main (Caesar's) tower rising to 147 feet. The Capability Brown gardens provide a superb setting.

After exploring the castle and grounds, leave by the main entrance to arrive in **Castle Hill**, where you go right and then right again down **Mill Street** to enjoy a classic view of the magnificent castle. Retrace your steps to **Castle Hill** and go right along the pavement onto **Castle Bridge**, from where you will have the most photographed view of the

THE WATERMAN, HATTON

castle. Return to the Warwick side of the bridge and cross over the busy **A425 Banbury Road** with great care.

Now descend the steps to the footpath and walk by the side of the **River Avon** towards **Leamington Spa**, keeping to the pathway for about a mile. Immediately after going beneath the aqueduct go left and climb the steps onto the towpath of the **Grand Union Canal**. To enjoy a fine view over the river and to see the place where the **River Leam** meets the **River Avon**, go left onto the aqueduct; then retrace your steps to the towpath. (2 miles)

② Walk along the towpath in the direction of **Warwick** as far as **Hatton Junction**. The **Waterman Inn** is a short distance from Hatton Junction. (4 miles)

The Warwick and Birmingham Canal was opened in 1799 to carry coal to Warwick and Leamington Spa. It later was used for transporting cargoes of tomato purée for the HP factory in nearby Birmingham and for carrying newsprint and buffalo hides. It became part of the Grand Union Canal Company, which was formed in 1932 to ensure the continuing success of the canal network. During the Second World War, the Grand Union Canal was one of but a few key routes where women were drafted in to run the boats after many of the men were conscripted into the forces. They made an attractive sight along the canal, with their shawls, blouses, long skirts, and pleated and frilled bonnets to protect them from the rain and the sun.

③ Cross canal **bridge 54** and go ahead over the stile onto a clear footpath into open countryside. Cross the bridge over the mainline railway and continue along the path over a couple of cultivated fields. Soon you cross pastureland, keeping to the left of **Budbrooke Farm**. Follow the clear waymarkers past the farm complex and walk along the farm track past a farm cottage. The track bends left and soon you will reach a lane. Here, fork right and, passing attractive houses, go into **Budbrooke**.

In the 14th century, the village fell victim to the Black Death, and the railway arch near to the village, known as Kytes Bridge, is believed to stand on the route taken to carry plague corpses from the village to Dead Field on Hatton Hill. The medieval village was burnt down to eradicate the disease, with the result that St Michael's church is detached from the modern village.

Later, the Budbrooke estate was a great supplier of timber to

Henry VIII, and much of this was used in the rebuilding of Warwick Castle.

The village had a long association with the Royal Warwickshire Regiment, which was formed in 1674 and served with much distinction in a series of wars. Budbrooke barracks were opened in 1877 to become the home of the Royal Warwickshire Fusiliers, the regiment of Field Marshall Montgomery of Alamein. Sadly, 1960 saw the closure of the barracks, and on 23rd April 1968, the regiment was merged with the Royal Northumberland and Lancashire Fusiliers to become the Royal Regiment of Fusiliers.

Spare time to visit **St Michael's church**, and then walk through the car park and go over the stile onto a footpath going in a south-easterly direction towards **Hampton Magna**. The footpath arcs right past a pond to arrive on **Old Budbrooke Road**. You will pass near to a memorial to the Royal Warwickshire Regiment on the edge of the village. Walk the fenced/hedged footpath that goes to the left of the houses and leads down to the very busy **A46**. Cross over the **A46** with very great care and continue over pastureland until you enter the area of **Warwick Racecourse** via a footbridge. Go ahead, enjoying the fine view over **Warwick town**. You will pass to the right of the golf course as you return to the car park area. (3 miles)

Date walk completed:

NAPTON ON THE HILL AND THE CANAL

THE OXFORD CANAL, NEAR NAPTON ON THE HILL

Distance:
9 miles

Starting Point:
St Lawrence's
Church car park
in Napton on the
Hill. GR 463610

Maps: OS Explorer 206 Edge Hill and Fenny Compton, OS
Explorer 222 Rugby and Daventry

How to get there: *Napton on the Hill is situated off the
A425, some 13 miles east of Warwick.*

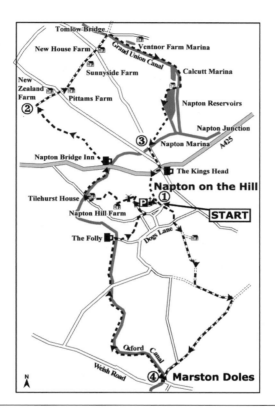

This figure-of-eight walk starts from the beautiful village of Napton on the Hill, which is dominated by a fine landmark windmill. The route takes you past the windmill and descends past the Napton Bridge Inn, by the Grand Union Canal, into beautiful countryside. After walking along some good tracks, you pick up the towpath by the canal, passing two very busy marinas, where there are many colourful narrowboats to admire, as you progress to lunchtime refreshments along the banks of the picturesque Napton reservoirs. The route then climbs to the hilltop, descends through Napton on the Hill village, and crosses agricultural land to a 'white' lane to reach the Grand Union Canal once again, in Marston Doles. The walk concludes with a fine view of the windmill from the towpath, passing the Folly Inn on the return to Napton on the Hill.

As you walk along the towpath of the Grand Union Canal you may spot the notice inviting 'captains and galley slaves' to desert their galleys and visit the pub, the pub in question being the **Kings Head** – and walkers are equally welcome; you will not be disappointed.

Hot, filled baguettes or a full restaurant meal is the choice. Steaks are a speciality of the pub and the steak bomb (meat heated up with peppers, mushrooms and onions) is very special. If you don't like it too hot, there is always the excellent carvery or you may be tempted by the specials boards. Hook Norton beers ('Best' and 'Old') are on tap in this friendly pub, where children and dogs all receive a warm welcome. There is a garden with plenty of benches and tables where you can enjoy refreshment in a relaxed atmosphere. The opening times from Monday to Friday are 12 noon to 3 pm and 5.30 pm to 11 pm; and on Saturday and Sunday the pub is open all day from 12 noon to 11 pm. Food is available every day from 12 noon to 3 pm and from 6 pm to 9 pm. Telephone: 01926 812202.

 The Walk

① Start your walk by strolling along the lane past the church and its second, smaller car park until you reach a lane junction. Bear right at the junction and go along the driveway towards the windmill – the building and land are private, so please keep off the property. Go right at the entrance (by the 'private' sign) along a footpath and follow the waymarkers. This leads to lovely open land and you now begin a descent of **Napton Hill**. At the junction of paths, bear left and go towards **Napton Hill Farm**, turning right in front of the farm and walking along the path that arcs right along the fence line. In about 250 yards where the path

bends sharp left, you descend gently towards some delightful fishing pools. Stay by the fence and go over the stile by the side of **Tilehurst House** onto a lane. Head right down the lane for about 100 yards and then cross **bridge 112** over the **Oxford Canal** by **Napton Bridge Inn**.

The Oxford Canal is a contour canal that clings to the line to the west of Napton on the Hill. It was started by James Brindley and completed after his death by Samuel Simcock. The original intention was to carry coal southwards from the Warwickshire coalfields to Banbury and Oxford. The walk takes you along the towpath of two short stretches of the canal and past the spectacle of Napton Locks.

Find the stile and waymarker to the left of the inn and go over this into open countryside. Over the first three fields you will be walking along a path to the right of the field hedge and you will then cross a large cultivated field, following small ground posts in a north-westerly direction and going over a further stile with **New Zealand Farm** to your right. At the end of the next field you will reach a track before a farm gate and a stile. (2 miles)

② Turn right along the track (do not go over the stile) and walk north-eastwards, passing to the right of **New Zealand Farm** to reach a road. Cross over the road and continue ahead up the driveway towards **Pittams Farm**. The track goes to the left of the buildings and goes diagonally left, passing by a plantation of young trees. After passing to the left of **Sunnyside Farm**, cross another road and continue ahead, going to the left of **New House Farm** and crossing an old railway bridge to reach **Tomlow Bridge** over the **Grand Union Canal**.

The Grand Union Canal is 137 miles long, stretching from the River Thames at Brentford to

---

THE KINGS HEAD ON THE GRAND UNION CANAL

reach Birmingham and passing through 166 locks. Boatmen used to claim to be able to travel the whole length of the canal in five days but allowed well over a week if they wanted to get any sleep!

Descend to the towpath and turn right, towards **Napton on the Hill**. There follows an easy stretch of walking along the towpath. You will pass by two marinas, **Ventnor Farm** and **Calcutta**, and should spare time to watch the colourful narrowboats. Just after passing by **Calcutta Marina** you will pass some lock gates.

Cross over the canal near to the canal shop (on the far side of the canal) and bear left, then right, to walk around the **Napton reservoirs**. If you are lucky you may see a fisherman catching tench, carp, or roach, and you are almost sure to see ducks, coots, and other waterfowl on the reservoirs. As you approach the end of the last reservoir, look out for a stile down the bank to your right. Go over this and the footbridge; then continue by walking on the clear footpath over the next three fields. (2¼ miles)

③ When you reach the road, turn left and continue until you meet the **A425** in the village of **Napton on the Hill**; the **King's Head** is opposite.

The windmill and the church buildings at Napton on the Hill have been local landmarks for centuries. Set high on a hilltop above the houses of the village, they can be seen for many miles and on a clear day one can see seven counties from the top of the hill. Not surprisingly the name of the village is thought to mean 'settlement (Old English tun) on a hill shaped like an inverted bowl (Old English knæpp)'. Below the 750-year-old church, the village is a pleasing mix of thatched, stone cottages and more modern houses. The windmill is now in private ownership, and sadly its arms are unlikely to do other than stretch out against the skyline.

Walk along the pavement of the **A425** into the village and go left through a kissing gate to climb **Napton Hill** on a hedged footpath (on a hot day you may be glad to have the shelter). As you approach the top of the hill, the path passes through three metal kissing gates to reach open land once again and the lane to **St Lawrence's church**. Cross over the lane, proceed through a hand gate, and descend the waymarked hedged footpath, passing **Arlington House** to reach **Vicarage Road**. Go right along the road for 50 yards and then turn left down **Godsons Lane** into **Dogs Lane**. Here, go right for 50 yards and then head left along a hedged bridleway going in a south-easterly direction away from the village. Continue for about 350 yards through a series of farm gates. After going through the sixth farm gate, turn left and proceed by the field edge over three fields.

At the junction of footpaths turn right along a 'white' lane (a farm track), walking now in a south-westerly direction for almost a mile. To the left you will pass **Potash Farm** before arriving at a lane corner; here go along the lane maintaining your direction, to reach **Welsh Road** by the **Oxford Canal** at **Marston Doles**. (2³/₄ miles)

④ Turn right and descend to the towpath, heading northwards towards **Napton**. You will walk past some fine lock gates and may want to get your camera ready for a photo opportunity as narrowboats make their way along the canal. Just after going beneath **bridge 116**, there is an exceptional view of

Napton and the windmill sitting proudly on high. Continue along the towpath to **bridge 113**, where you can visit the **Folly Inn**.

Being situated on the towpath, the Folly Inn, once called the Bull and Butcher, is a popular place with boaters and walkers and is well-known for its home-cooked pies – a nice place to sink a pint on a hot day.

Cross over **bridge 113** into **Folly Lane**, and in about 30 yards go left over a stile/footbridge to cross the meadowland and a second footbridge. Walk along a track to a stile. Follow the direction of the waymarkers and diagonally cross a large field to a final stile onto **Poplar Road** in the village.

Go right along the road for 80 yards and then turn left up **Hollow Way Lane**. This leads to the lane junction near to **Church Leys Farm**, where you go right to return to the car park. (2 miles)

Date walk completed:

WINDMILLS ON THE MIND AT HARBURY

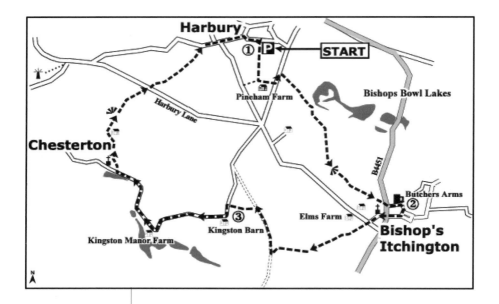

Distance:
7 miles

Starting Point:
The village car park in Constance Drive, Harbury. GR 373597

Map: OS Explorer 206 Edge Hill and Fenny Compton

How to get there: *Harbury is 7 miles south-east of Warwick. It is best approached via the B4455 (Fosse Way). Middle Road leads into the village and you will find the car park in South Parade.*

CHESTERTON WINDMILL

*T*he route takes you across gentle farmland and past Bishops Bowl Lakes, where dinosaur fossils were unearthed. You pass by lakes and pools on the way to Chesterton village to see its lovely old church and you will be intrigued by its windmill (well worth a visit), which overlooks the local landscape from a nearby hilltop.

Pub spotting could offer a pleasant diversion in Harbury. You may perhaps choose to locate the Crown Inn in Crown Street, the Gamecock on the corner of Chapel Street, the Dog Inn, the Old New Inn in Temple End, and The Shakespeare, a 16th-century, timber-framed inn situated near to an 18th-century windmill, now without sails.

You will enjoy a visit to the friendly **Butcher's Arm** in Bishop Itchington, where you will receive a warm welcome. This Pubmaster pub has a reputation for good food, well-kept real ales and a value-for-money wine list. The opening hours are from midday to 3 pm and from 5.30 pm to 11 pm during the week. On Saturday it is open all day from noon and on Sunday the evening opening is from 7 pm to 10.30 pm.

Greene King, Abbot Ale and a guest beer are the real ales to enjoy in the cosy bar with its lovely open fire. You can eat from a good choice of home-cooked food in the separate dining room. Good pub food is available between noon and 2 pm each day (3 pm on Saturday), and in the evening food is available between 7 pm (5.30 pm on Saturdays) and 10 pm during the week. The hot bacon baguettes provide a welcome snack during a longer walk. If you prefer a hearty main meal, then perhaps the 24 oz rump steak will appeal. Alternatively you can select from pot meals, jacket potatoes and vegetarian options. Special children's meals are also available.

Children like the playground, and dogs under control are welcome. Telephone: 01926 614161.

 *The Walk*

① Leave the village hall car park by the footpath at the rear of the building and continue until you reach a junction of paths. Here, go left and pass **Pineham Farm** to arrive on a quiet road. Turn left and walk along the grass verge for about 120 yards. Then go right over a stile into open countryside and take the clear footpath set to the left of the field hedge, going in a south-easterly direction. In about 350 yards you will reach a stile onto a wide track where you can go left up to the edge of the **Bishops Bowl Lakes** for a good view of the lakes and the wild birds that congregate on them.

Retrace your steps and continue walking to the left of the field hedge.

The lakes and pools known as Bishops Bowl Lakes were once stone quarries which yielded up some dinosaur fossils, now held in the Natural History Museum in South Kensington. The area is now much enjoyed by ornithologists and local fishermen.

After some 250 yards the path bears right and you diagonally cross the next large field. At its corner, go over a further stile and continue, walking to the left of the field hedge (again in a south-easterly direction), with the village of **Bishop's Itchington** ahead; the church is clearly visible and beyond this you can see the stone turret on the **Burton Dassett Hills**. Continue to the village, walking on a tarmac hedged path past houses to arrive on **Station Road** (the **B4451**). The **Butchers Arms** pub is in **Fisher Road** opposite. (2 miles)

Bishops Itchington is an unassuming village, with the church of St Michael standing proud on the skyline. It was built in 1872 on the site of the original All Saints' church but now serves as a private residence.

The village came to public notice in 1949 when a parish council could not be formed because only one man offered himself for election. A Mrs Chapel Hyam and six members of the W.I. stood for election and were elected to form what the press dubbed 'the petticoat government' of Bishops Itchington.

② Continue past the pub and go through the small shopping area in the village to arrive via **Chapel Street** back on the **B4451**, which you cross. Walk up **Manor Road**, going to the left of **St Michael's**

THE BUTCHERS ARMS, BISHOPS ITCHINGTON

church. At the junction go ahead over a stile into open countryside once again, with **Elms Farm** visible to your right. Go over the stile at the end of the first field and follow the direction of the waymarker, going to the right into a small area of trees. Diagonally cross the next field, aiming for its far left-hand corner and continue ahead (east). At the next hedge bear slightly left on a taped track to reach the field hedge and a junction of tracks.

Turn right and head up the wide track; you will be walking on part of the **Centenary Way**, going generally north and then north-west.

The Centenary Way is a 98-mile walkway that runs from Kingsbury Water Park to Upper Quinton. It winds through quiet and low-lying countryside, beside canals, through numerous country parks, up Burton Dassett Hills and Edge Hill, and passes through the towns of Kenilworth, Warwick, Leamington Spa and Shipston-on-Stour, connecting at each end with the Heart of England Way. It was inaugurated by the county council to celebrate its centenary in 1989 and was opened in 1991.

In about 600 yards turn left and walk along the footpath to the left of the field hedge. Ahead you will see **Kingston Barn** and surrounding

buildings. Continue up to the driveway/track to these buildings and then head left along the driveway/lane passing to the right of them. (2^1/$_4$ miles)

③ Turn right to continue along the lane heading east. This pleasant stretch leads in half a mile or so to a road junction by **Kingston Manor** Farm; up to your left you will see and hear the busy **M40** motorway. Turn right and continue along the lane, passing some attractive small lakes and pools to your left. The lane bends right and then left, to become a clear tarmac road as you approach the village of **Chesterton** and its church.

St Giles' church is inextricably linked with the Peyto family. Sir Edward Peyto supported Cromwell's Parliamentarians and successfully led the defence of Warwick Castle against the Royalists – as ever, it was good to be on the winning side. The oldest part of the building is the 14th-century nave. The ornamental gateway in the north wall to the left was designed by Inigo Jones and built to provide a suitable entry for the Peyto family when attending church.

Leave the churchyard through the hand gate at its rear and cross the field, going over the footbridge in the hedge below. Go through the next field, aiming to the left of some rather derelict buildings (in the valley to the left are the buildings of **Lodge Farm**). To the south-west of these buildings are the remains of a medieval settlement called **Netherend**, which is mentioned in a document of 1319.

As you progress you will be captivated by the appearance of the windmill on the horizon; this is **Chesterton Windmill**. (Unfortunately there are no footpaths to provide a link route to the windmill, but it is possible to visit it from a permissive path off a nearby road.)

Go through the hand gate and head right through a farm gate. A second hand gate leads into a large field, which you cross, aiming half right (north-east) towards a hand gate in the fence ahead; the site of the Peytos' manor house is to the left. Follow the waymark direction towards the corner of the next field to reach **Harbury Lane**. Cross over the lane and go ahead, maintaining your north-easterly direction over several fields and stiles until you emerge by a house in **Temple End** at the eastern end of **Harbury village**.

A huge ichthyosaurus lived at Harbury some hundred million years ago. Bronze Age cooking pots provide evidence of settlement in the area of this beautiful village, where later Roman legions would have been seen marching along the nearby Fosse Way. The village still has a school that was built in Shakespeare's day. Set behind the Norman church, Wagstaff School was founded in 1611, and a memorial to the founder, Jane Wagstaff, can be seen in the church. The Shakespeare Inn has graced the village for some 500 years and is popular with walkers.

Turn right along the pavement, passing the **Old New Inn** and the **Manor House** as you progress into **Park Lane** and then bear right into **South Parade** to return to the car park at the back of the village hall. ($2^3/_4$ miles)

 Date walk completed:

ALCESTER WAYS TO THE VILLAGES

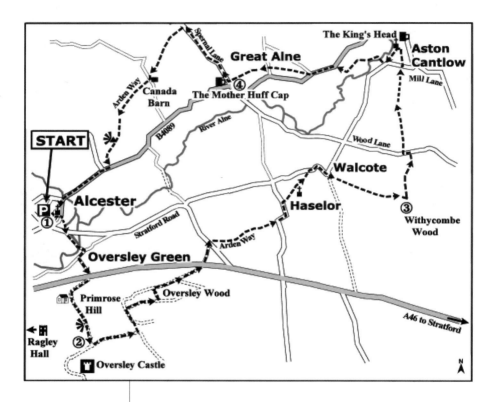

Distance:
11 miles

Starting Point:
Bulls Head Yard car park in Alcester.
GR 088573

Map: OS Explorer 205 Stratford-upon-Avon and Evesham

How to get there: *Alcester is 8 miles west of Stratford-upon-Avon. The town is best approached on the A46 from Stratford-upon-Avon. In 6 miles, turn right onto the Stratford road, which will take you past Oversley Green into Alcester. Turn right down High Street and follow the signs to the car park, which is situated off School Road.*

THE ALMSHOUSES IN ALCESTER

*T*his is an easy pleasant walk, venturing into Roman Alcester and surrounding villages. The walk passes through lovely woods and pretty villages where beautiful thatched cottages add to the rural scene. In spring, wild flowers adorn a number of the footpaths and the woods abound with bluebells.

The route follows an attractive part of the Heart of England Way, passing through Oversley Wood and linking with the Arden Way (a circular walk around the Forest of Arden area of the county, starting in the nearby medieval town of Henley in Arden). You will pass through the picturesque villages of Haselor and Watcote to reach Aston Cantlow.

Swathed in Virginia creeper, the beautiful 15th-century **King's Head** is part of our literary history for it is said that the parents of William Shakespeare held their wedding breakfast here after the ceremony in the nearby church of St John the Baptist. The interior is full of old world character with oak beams, oak furniture and settles, stone-flagged floors and gleaming brasses. In winter you can indulge yourself by the open fire, sitting in the huge inglenook or in one of the hidden corners. Outside there is a massive spreading chestnut tree.

The food menu offers good value, traditional pub fare, with the accent on flavour, texture and colour. You can eat in the restaurant or in the large garden, which has plenty of benches and tables. The quality real ales sold are Brew XI, Blacksheep and Abbots Ale, with Dry Blackthorn cider also on draught. The opening hours are 11 am to 3 pm and 5.30 pm to 11 pm from Monday to Friday, and all day at weekends from 11 am to 11 pm on Saturday and from 12 noon to 10.30 pm on Sunday. Telephone: 01789 488242. Fax. 01789 488137.

The Walk

Picturesque Malt Mill Lane is one of the most photographed lanes in Warwickshire.

① From **Bulls Head Yard** bear left through one of the passageways into **Alcester's High Street**. Turn left and then right past **St Nicholas's church**. At the corner, turn right down **Malt Mill Lane**, taking time to stroll through the delightful gardens to the right.

Alcester is an old market town standing at the junction of two Roman roads. It later became a well known coaching town, and although some of the ancient coaching inns have disappeared it has maintained an old world appearance, with many timber-fronted houses and a superb timber-topped town hall.

At the bottom of the lane, bear left through the small park area by the **River Arrow** to reach and cross over **Stratford Road**. Go down the road opposite into the village of **Oversley Green**, passing by the football ground and crossing the old river bridge. At the junction turn right and soon you will be walking past some charming thatched cottages. Turn left up **Primrose Lane**, passing probably the most beautiful thatched cottages in the Midlands. Cross the footbridge over the **A46** road and then go right and climb **Primrose Hill**. At **Lower Oversley Lodge Farm**, bear left and continue along the good farm track (this is part of the **Heart of England Way**).

As you progress you will enjoy a fine view of **Ragley Hall** to your right and the white building of **Oversley Castle** ahead of you. (1¹/₂ miles)

Ragley Hall dates back to the year 710. It is the seat of the Marquess of Hertford, whose family has owned the land since 1591. Many fine paintings are displayed in the magnificent interior and a large fresco adorns the main entrance stairway. The 500-acre park, which includes a lovely lake, was landscaped by Capability Brown.

② Where the track bends right, turn left to arrive by the corner of **Oversley Wood**. Walk along the clear track inside the trees and then at the junction of paths, go left into the wood to reach the main forest track. Bear left along the forest track for about 100 yards then turn right. As this track descends, go left and you will soon be going down to rejoin the main forest track, where you turn right. Go along the track and leave the wood, bearing left beneath the **A46** road bridge and walk along the lane to the junction with **Stratford Road**. Cross the road and bear left for about 30 yards; then go right over a stile to join the **Arden Way**. Follow the waymarkers, keeping to the field edge path until

THE KING'S HEAD, ASTON CANTLOW

you arrive at the corner of a lane in the village of **Haselor**. Go ahead along the lane, and then left through the village.

Opposite the old post office, go right through a bridlegate by the village noticeboard and the three-person stocks.

Haselor has a watermill (Hoo Mill) which was used by the lord of the manor to grind corn; today it is used to press apples to make cider. The stocks were last used in 1841, to punish local boys who trampled down a field of corn.

Go through a farm gate and then climb the hill and pass through **Haselor** churchyard to reach the lane. Go right and stroll through the attractive hamlet of **Walcote**. At the second sharp bend go ahead onto a farm track and then go left over the stile opposite **Dinglewood Cottage**. Now walk along the field-edge footpath up to **Withycombe Wood**. (3³/₄ miles)

③ Turn left along the footpath inside the wood and continue through a bridlegate into a field, crossing this field to a further bridlegate onto **Wood Lane**. Go left along the lane for about 50 yards and then cross over and go right, crossing a stile into a field. The footpath joins a farm track by a small conifer plantation and continues to **Mill Lane** at a sign for

Aston Cantlow. Cross the lane, go over the stile opposite and cross the next field to a plank bridge into the **churchyard of St John the Baptist**. The **King's Head** pub is just beyond the church gate.

Aston Cantlow is a delightful village to wander around, with a number of old buildings worthy of attention; the beautiful half-timbered village hall is opposite the King's Head, and situated on the edge of the village is Billesley Manor, now a hotel, which was once owned by the Trussell family. The last Trussell was hanged as a highwayman during the reign of Elizabeth I. In 1557 William Shakespeare's parents were married in the lovely church here.

Return to the churchyard and follow the path to the left of the church, passing to the right of the **Old School**. Pass through the lovely archway of trees to the road, where you turn right and go past a caravan park. Turn right down the footpath to the left of the park entrance, cross the footbridge over the **River Alne**, and then bear left until you go beneath an old railway bridge. Go right and take the good track/lane up to the **B4089** on the edge of **Great Alne**. Turn left and head along the road. At the entrance to an industrial estate, bear right onto a footpath crossing a field to reach a fenced path. Turn left and go along the back of village houses. In just over 1¼ miles you will arrive on **Spernal Lane** by the **Mother Huff Cap** pub. (3¼ miles)

Great Alne is a village of attractive houses which line the B4089 road near to the River Alne. The Mother Huff Cap is a favourite haunt for local walkers, and is mentioned in verse:

> *Twixt Michaelmas and Martinmas*
> *Old dame began to brew,*
> *With half a pint of old malt*
> *And half a pint of new.*
> *First twenty gallons of Huff my*
> *   Cap,*
> *Then twenty gallons worse than*
> *   that,*
> *Then twenty gallons as amber*
> *   clear,*
> *And then she brewed the*
> *   servants' beer.*

④ Turn right and head up **Spernal Lane** for about ¾ mile and by **New End Cottages** turn left. Cross over the footbridge and follow the **Heart of England Way**. In about 500 yards, cross over the farm track to reach a pond via the stile opposite.

Now go down to the right, passing to the right of **Canada Barn** to reach **Coughton Fields Lane**. Go left along the lane for 25 yards and then go right through a farm gate onto a wide farm track. The track becomes a path as the route progresses over a stile and veers left over a further stile. Go right, cross the old bridge over the dismantled railway, and go through the hand gates before bearing right onto a path crossing a large cultivated field. Here you pass a trig point (an impressive 201 ft) which offers a good view over **Alcester**. Go over the stile at the end of the field and descend left through trees to reach the **B4089** in **Alcester**.

Now go right and walk along the pavement into the town centre, passing the **Greig Memorial Hall** on the right and then crossing the bridge over the **River Arrow**. Go up **Henley Street**, bearing right past the beautiful old town hall. Pass **St Nicholas's church** and stroll through quaint **Butter Street** to reach **High Street**. Go right through the alleyway to return to the car park. (2½ miles)

Date walk completed:

STRATFORD-UPON-AVON AND THE SHIRE HORSE CENTRE

THE ROYAL SHAKESPEARE THEATRE, STRATFORD-UPON-AVON

Distance:
7¹/₄ miles

Starting Point:
Recreation ground car park in Stratford-upon-Avon.
GR 204546

Map: OS Explorer 205 Stratford-upon-Avon and Evesham

How to get there: *Stratford-upon-Avon is situated some 8 miles south-west of Warwick. Leave Warwick on the A429 going onto the A46. In 4 miles bear left onto the A439 into Stratford. Go left to join the A3400 and left again to cross Clopton Bridge then circle the island to enter the car park by the River Avon.*

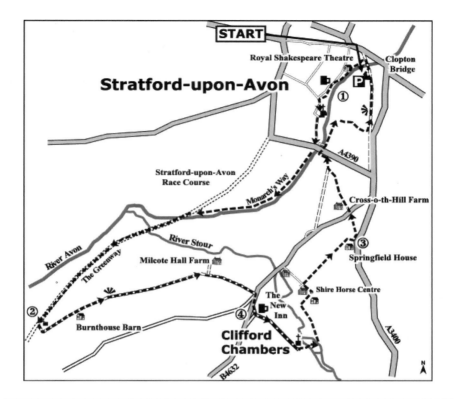

*T*his lovely walk offers the opportunity to explore William Shakespeare's Stratford. You will pass the Royal Shakespeare Theatre and Holy Trinity church and then continue along the banks of the River Avon. As you approach Clifford Chambers there are good views of Stratford and the surrounding countryside. Clifford Chambers is a picturesque village, set back from the main road, and, passing in front of the manor house, you will traverse its attractive main street. After crossing a footbridge over the River Stour, you come to the Shire Horse Centre, where you will be enchanted by the magnificent animals enjoying the freedom of the countryside. The return route passes near to a fine old farmhouse before gently going down to the River Avon and concludes with a stroll past the Avon weir before ascending onto the old tramway by the Butterfly Centre.

The New Inn is a delightful 400-year-old coaching inn, which is sited at the very entrance to the picturesque village of Clifford Chambers; it stands close to the B4632, which was once an important route leading on to Gloucester and the south-west. This family run inn offers a log fire, a separate non-smoking restaurant, a beer garden, and a children's area.

Bass is the real ale on tap and there are extensive menus for the restaurant and bar. The New Inn is well known among local walkers for its superb home-cooked food, which is all freshly prepared to order. You may eat in the quaint bar with open log fire, in the non-smoking restaurant, or in the conservatory restaurant, and there are tables and benches for those who want to eat outside. If you prefer an evening meal, can I suggest Wednesday or Saturday, for the carvery is excellent. I am a pudding man and choosing a dessert can be difficult: whether to have the delicious homemade bread and butter pudding or the scrumptious fruit crumble? This is a very popular pub and booking for Sunday lunch is essential. The opening hours are 12 noon to 3 pm and 6 pm to 11 pm from Monday to Friday and all day on Saturday and Sunday. B&B accommodation is available for those who wish to stop overnight. Email: thenewinn65@aol.com; telephone: 01789 293402.

The Walk

① From the car park, go past the old boathouse and cross the tramway bridge. Go left into the canal basin area and then keep to the pathway by the side of the **River Avon**. This will take you along the balcony of the **Royal Shakespeare Theatre** and into the theatre gardens; here you can enjoy a good view of the old part of the theatre building.

The famous Royal Shakespeare Theatre was built in 1932, although the back of the building is much older, and there are beautiful gardens that run down to the banks of the River Avon. The theatre is one of the most famous in the world, and many leading actors from Britain and elsewhere have performed on its proscenium arch stage.

Leave the gardens onto **Southern Lane**, opposite the **Black Swan** pub. Go left along the pavement past the ferry (which I used to work at lunchtime when crossing the River Avon to play minature golf on the waterside park). Go left again to enter **Avonside Gardens**. The path will take you past the **Brass Rubbing Centre** and you will soon arrive on the pavement in **Old Town**.

At the Brass Rubbing Centre, which is located in a 19th-century summerhouse, visitors can take their own rubbings from a superb collection of medieval and Tudor brass plaques that reflect England's unique heritage; there are knights and ladies, scholars, merchants, and priests of the past.

Up the road to the right is the fine building of Hall's Croft, perhaps the most impressive of the five Shakespeare properties in the town. Set on a stone foundation, it has a substantial oak frame with lath and plaster infill, and a tiled gabled roof, surmounted by attractive brick chimney stacks. This was the home of Dr John Hall and his wife Susanna, Shakespeare's elder daughter, who married in 1607. Dr Hall had his practice here and it was the couple's home until after Shakespeare's death. John and Susanna Hall are buried in the chancel of Holy Trinity church.

Walk back into **Old Town**, heading towards **Holy Trinity church** and walking down the tree-lined approach to the church.

THE NEW INN, CLIFFORD CHAMBERS

The beautiful parish church of Holy Trinity stands in attractive grounds on the banks of the River Avon and has a very fine steeple, which was erected in 1763. Inside is the burial place of William Shakespeare, who was baptised there in 1564 and died in April, 1616. His burial is recorded in the parish register – 'April 25 Will.Shakspere gent'. Shakepeare's tomb of simple stones is sited in front of the altar and is engraved with the following intriguing curse:

> *Good frend for Jesus sake forebeare*
> *To digg the dust enclosed heare!*
> *Bleste be the man that spares the stones*
> *And curst be he that moves my bones.*

Go into **Mill Lane** and continue down it, passing the old mill building which has been converted to apartments, to reach the **River Avon** by the **A4390**. Go under the fine bridge and walk along **Monarch's Way** footpath on the right bank of the **Avon**. In just under a mile you will reach an old railway bridge (**Stannels Bridge**) and here you ascend and go left onto the **Greenway**, which you follow for the next mile. (2³/₄ miles)

The Greenway is a former railway line that was used extensively by REME soldiers who were garrisoned at nearby Long Marston army camp. It is now a well-used recreational route offering several miles of easy walking in the Stratford area.

② At **Clifford Halt**, turn left and walk along the clear, wide bridleway past **Burnthouse Barn**, pausing from time to time to enjoy the scenic views of **Bordon Hill** to your left. After passing **Milcote Hall Farm** (about 1¹/₄ miles), you will soon arrive at the **B4632** road, with the **New Inn** and **Clifford Chambers** opposite. Passing the **New Inn**, go along the main street into the village. At its end you will see the fine manor house; here, go left onto a footpath that will lead you over a footbridge over the **River Stour** in front of an old mill.

Until early in the 20th century, Clifford Chambers belonged to the Abbey of St Peter of Gloucester and was in Gloucestershire; it came into Warwickshire following changes to the county boundary. The main street of the village is a long 'dead end' street lined with attractive timber-framed houses, and there is a tiny square of ancient cottages to admire. At the end of the main street is the splendid building of Clifford Manor, which William Shakespeare together with his friends Michael Drayton and Ben Jonson frequently visited. There were several branches of the

Shakespeare family living in the village in the mid 16th century.

Continue along the marked footpath, bearing left over a second footbridge to arrive at the **Shire Horse Centre**.

Magnificent shire horses appear to be everywhere as you walk through the pastureland at the back of the Shire Horse Centre and Farm Park. Here you can experience the country life of the past, with working Shire horses, wagon rides, farm animals, including rare breeds, and 'The Country Village Experience'. There is also a good café if you are ready for light refreshment. Telephone: 01789 415274.

Cross over the pastureland at the centre and then bear right to walk between the buildings. Bear right and go through the farm gate onto a footpath which continues half right (in a north-easterly direction). In just under half a mile you will go past **Springfield House**. (3 miles)

③ Here, bear half left, crossing the field to reach a stile onto the **B4632** road. Cross the road with care and go along the footpath that passes

between the buildings of **Cross-o-th'-Hill Farm**. The path goes downhill past trees to reach a tarmac path. Bear right onto this and descend to a stile below the **A4390**. Go left along the footpath to the banks of the **River Avon** near to the road bridge. Pass underneath the bridge and bear right to walk along the river bank and past the weir, with **Holy Trinity church** adding to the view.

Just after going over a small stone bridge, turn right and take the clear path that leads up onto the old tramway. Go left along the tramway, taking in the fine view over the recreation area and cricket pitch. You will pass the **Butterfly Centre** before arriving back at the car park. (1½ miles)

A visit to Europe's largest butterfly farm offers the opportunity to see some of the world's most spectacular and colourful species as they fly around you. You can walk amongst hundreds of exotic butterflies in a rainforest environment, with tropical plants and waterfalls. Children enjoy seeing the ants, beetles and stick insects in their 'natural' habitats, safely behind glass!

Date walk completed:

DORSINGTON AND THE SHAKESPEARE VILLAGES

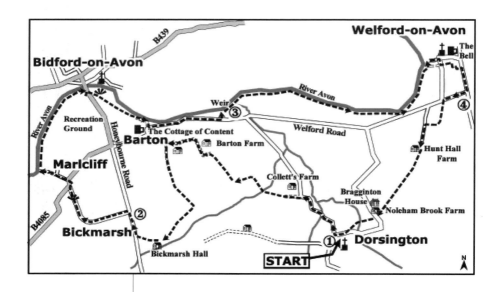

Distance:
11 miles

Map: OS Explorer 205 Stratford-upon-Avon and Evesham

Starting Point:
*The church in Dorsington.
GR 132497*

How to get there: *Dorsington is 16 miles south-west of Warwick. From Stratford take the B439 road towards Evesham and in 3¹/₂ miles go left into Welford-on-Avon. At the end of High Street head right along Barton Road and in ¹/₂ mile go left into Braggington Lane, following the signs to reach Dorsington. Park with consideration near to the church.*

THE WEIR ON THE RIVER AVON AT BARTON

*T*his walk explores the Shakespeare connection. You pass through several picturesque villages associated with the Shakespeare family and walk along the banks of the River Avon. The beautiful hamlet of Marlcliff greets you with a profusion of snowdrops in early spring. The 13th-century Falcon Inn, opposite the church in Bidford-upon-Avon, was one of the Bard's favourite taverns. He is reputed to have got drunk at this inn and slept it off under an apple tree. You can share the fine view he no doubt enjoyed from Bidford Bridge before proceeding to the Cottage of Content for refreshments. In Welford-on-Avon, thatched cottages line the streets and its famous maypole will catch the eye before you return to open countryside on the way back to the village of Dorsington.

Situated in the tiny hamlet of Barton, the **Cottage of Content** is a regular haunt of walkers in the area and customers can be sure of a warm welcome. This low-beamed, timber-framed pub is situated close to the river and Barton Lock. The bar is open from 11 am to 2.30 pm and 6 pm to 11 pm from Monday to Saturday, and on Sunday from noon to 3 pm and 7 pm to 10.30 pm. There is a wide range of traditional ales to choose from: draught Bass, Tetley Bitter, Boddingtons, Carlsberg, Grolsch, or Guinness; or perhaps Strongbow cider will appeal. The pub is renowned for its good home-cooked food and generous portions. The bar food menu offers a broad selection, from sandwiches to full à la carte, and you can eat in one of the gardens or you may prefer the cosy restaurant. Food is available between 12 noon and 2 pm with evening meals between 6 pm and 10 pm. Children are made very welcome; dogs are allowed in the garden only. Telephone: 01789 772279.

The Walk

Dorsington is a small, peaceful village tucked away in the Cotswold countryside. There are many lovely old thatched cottages and other interesting buildings to be found there. The seat around the oak tree in front of the church of St Peter always leaves me in doubt as to where I should sit.

① From the church in **Dorsington**, go up to the main road by the post office and then turn right along a lane for almost ¹/₂ mile. At the second bend in the lane, go along the **Heart of England Way** through a farm gate and onto a track, with **Collett's Farm** on your right. Continue through a second gate and follow the waymarkers as the track initially proceeds to the right of the hedge and then continues on the left to reach a large orchard. In about 250 yards, go right up the field edge by the orchard and approach **Barton Farm**, where you go to the left of the buildings, bearing left and soon right by the left side of the hedge. As the fruit packing station comes into view, go left at the field corner and walk along the good stone track to the right of the packing station buildings.

About 150 yards beyond the building, turn left onto a grass track, walking in a generally southerly direction. The track eventually reduces to a path by the side of a hedge and you walk over three fields. At the next field corner go through the gap in the fence and then bear right, aiming for **Bickmarsh Hall** with its huge grain silos. The path veers to the right of the buildings and you soon arrive on **Honeybourne Road**, the Roman road known as **Ryknield Street**. (3¹/₂ miles)

② Now turn right, walking along the grass verge for about 300 yards and passing the roadside houses in **Bickmarsh**. Head left into **Bickmarsh Lane** and continue along to the hamlet of **Marlcliff**. Along the way a fine view of the surrounding countryside unfolds as you descend to the road junction in **Marlcliff**. Go right along the **B4085** road for some 80 yards and then go left down the lane into the centre of the hamlet. Where the dead-end lane bends to the right, go straight

ahead, passing by a delightful tiny thatched cottage and the corner house called **Woodpeckers** as you head towards the **River Avon**.

Just before the river turn right over a stile and walk the **Avon Valley Footpath** along the banks of the **River Avon**. You will go over a couple of stiles before arriving in the recreation ground and **Honeybourne Road** by **Bidford Bridge**.

Although Bidford-on-Avon dates back to Saxon times it will remain forever famous as the place where Shakespeare got drunk – he is believed to have done this

THE COTTAGE OF CONTENT, BARTON

at the Falcon Inn and to have slept it off under a nearby crab-apple tree on his way back home. The town comprises stone and timber cottages, an old bridge, some attractive gardens, and a number of pleasant byways that have changed little since Shakespeare's day. Shakespeare would have stood on the eight arch bridge (one of Warwickshire's oldest bridges) and must have attended the lovely St Lawrence church that stands so proudly on the banks of the river. Its tower is 750-years-old and from its top one can look down over the bridge where the poet would have stood to gather his thoughts while looking out over the River Avon.

Cross the road and go over the stile opposite into pastureland. Follow the waymarkers of the **Heart of England Way** (see Walk 2) on a clear footpath that diagonally crosses three fields, pausing to enjoy the delightful view of **Bidford-on-Avon** over the river, with a weir and lock forming an interesting picture to your left. You will go over a couple of stiles as you proceed in a south-easterly direction and will soon be following the bank of the **Avon**. As you near the lock go right into a hedged green lane and go through a gate to reach the **B4085** once again at a corner of the road by the **Cottage of Content**. (3 miles)

③ Leaving the **Heart of England Way**, turn left onto the **B4085**; follow it for about ¹/₂ mile and then go left through a gateway to reach the **Avon's** banks. Take the **Avon Valley** footpath by the side of the river for the next 1¹/₂ miles and then head right to a stile onto a good path through the trees. At the end of the woodland the path arcs left and you continue along the river bank into the village of **Welford-on-Avon**.

After going through a farm gate, the route takes you to the right of the old mill and you follow the waymarkers to cross the bottom of **Mill Lane** and arrive in **Boat Lane**. Head right up **Boat Lane**, taking time to enjoy the beautiful black and white cottages; look out especially for **Ten Penny Cottage**. Near the top of the lane is **St Peter's church** and here you go right along **Headland Road**. When you are opposite the top of **Mill Lane**, go left along a footpath at the back of houses. You will pass by the extension to the graveyard of **St Peter's church** and in about ¹/₄ mile you will arrive at a junction of paths. Go left up to **High Street** to emerge opposite **Maypole Wine Stores**, near the famous maypole. (2¹/₂ miles)

The delightful village of Welford-on-Avon is yet another of Shakespeare's haunts, and what a beautiful village it is. A large number of half-timbered thatched cottages take one back to the Bard's time, as do the ancient mill, the maypole, and the beautiful lychgate to the Norman church. There are three superb pubs in the village and perhaps the story of the Four Alls is the most engaging. In its porch you will find a curious old painting showing four characters:

> *The king who rules over all*
> *The parson who prays for all*
> *The soldier who fights for all*
> *The farmer who pays for all.*

④ Head right along **High Street**, then go right along **Bidford Road** for about 300 yards. Now go left up a hedged track into the countryside once again. This well-used local track will lead you through some bushes, at the end of which you go right through a farm gate and continue along the field edge, going generally westwards until you reach a stile onto a lane. Head left up the lane, which is the driveway to **Hunts Hall Farm**, and in about 350 yards you pass to the left of the farm complex.

Follow the clear waymarkers and continue over a series of fields, heading generally south-west. You will pass to the left of **Braggington House** and **Noleham Brook Farm** to arrive on a road. Cross the road and continue over the stile opposite, aiming generally to the left of the last house in the village of **Dorsington**. Go over the stile onto the road and head right into the village, where your car is parked. (2 miles)

Date walk completed:

COMPTON VERNEY - THE BIG HOUSE

THE NORMAN CHURCH OF ST MARY AND ST MARGARET, COMBROOK

Distance:
12 miles

Starting Point:
The layby near
Lighthorne Rough.
GR 322544

Maps: OS Explorer 205 Stratford-upon-Avon and Evesham, 206
Edge Hill and Fenny Compton

How to get there: *Combrook is 10 miles south of
Warwick. Leave Warwick on the A429 road. In
Wellesbourne go left onto the B4086 for about 2$^{1}/_{2}$ miles
and then go right onto the B4455 Fosse Way. In just over
a mile go right onto a local road with Lighthorne Rough on
your left. At the first junction, go right and at the end of
the trees turn into the layby on the right.*

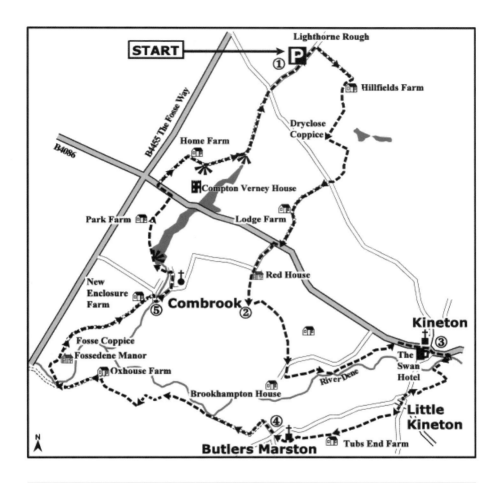

The walk starts north of the Compton Verney, a classical 18th-century mansion designed by Robert Adam, and crosses delightful rolling countryside to reach Kineton village, where refreshments are available at the Swan Hotel. From there the route goes on to Little Kineton and Butlers Marston, then passes by Fossedene Manor House on the way into Combrook village with its fine church and many thatched properties. A stroll through the park takes you past Compton Verney House.

The Swan Hotel was a coaching inn in the early 17th century and during the 19th century the Court of Petty Sessions regularly sat here. It has also served as a library and meeting place for many Kineton organizations. There is a very fine skittle alley and a newly developed beer garden. Inside you can relax in front of the open fireplaces and you can be sure of a warm welcome.

The opening hours are from 11.30 am to 3 pm during the week and from 5 pm to 11 pm in the evening. On Saturday the hotel is open for drinks all day between 11.30 am and 11 pm, while on Sunday it is open between noon and 10.30 pm. Pies, salads, bar snacks and sandwiches are served between noon and 2.30 pm during the week and from 6 pm to 9 pm each evening. On Sunday food is served at lunchtime only, between noon and 3 pm.

Website: www.pub-explorer.com; email: pftormey@aol.com; telephone: 01926 640876.

 *The Walk*

① From the layby near to **Lighthorne Rough**, walk towards the road junction (north-east) and turn right along the farm drive towards **Hillfields Farm**. Immediately in front of Hillfields Farm, turn right onto a bridlepath that skirts around the farm buildings and follow it south to a gap in the hedge by a stream.

Cross over the stream and climb a large field, aiming for a gap in the hedge to the left of **Dryclose Coppice**; then cross the next field on the path to arrive at **Kineton Road**, the **B4086**. Go right along the road for about 100 yards, and then go left along the lane towards **Red House**. At the lane corner, bear right and then go left up the signed footpath to the left of the house, walking in a southerly direction. (2³/₄ miles)

② Near to Hampton House Farm, turn left along a good headland path that arcs gently right by the side of the hedge as you progress around a large field. Go ahead over the driveway to **Brookhampton House** and continue by the hedge side for about 125 yards.

Go left over a stile and cross the next field then descend to a stile/footbridge. Continue to the left of a stream to reach the **B4086** in **Kineton**.

Wide streets and charming red and grey houses greet you in Kineton, where old inns and a lovely church provide a very English scene. In nearby Edgehill the banner of Charles I once waved over his army assembled for battle. The king addressed his troops, and Sir Jacob Astley, the commander of the infantry, cried: 'O Lord, Thou knowest how busy I must be this day: if I forget thee do not Thou forget me!' Kineton streets were blocked by carriages and wagons after the famous battle and the bells of the church tolled for the dead. Nine months later those bells rang out again for the king when he wed Henrietta Maria, the daughter of Henry IV of France.

Head right along the road as far as the junction in the middle of the village; the Swan Hotel is on the corner, near to the church. (2¹/₄ miles)

③ Bear right into **Banbury Street** and in about 250 yards go right again, crossing over the footbridge into open countryside. Following the waymarker direction, go right and follow the pleasant path set to the left of a stream. At the hedge go left and then go right on the path that leads to the left of the town's sports fields to arrive on the road on the edge of **Little Kineton**. Go left along the grass verge and into the village, bearing left onto **Tysoe Road** to reach the lovely village green.
    Leave the village green on the signed footpath to the left of the row of cottages, diagonally cross a small field to a stile, and then head

right along a hedged footpath going generally in a south-westerly direction. The footpath soon crosses pastureland and then passes to the right of **Tubs End Farm**. Go past the farm buildings and across the drive. Continue ahead on the footpath, crossing more pastureland to reach a lane across another stile. Go left along the lane and then bear right, passing to the left of **Butlers Marston church**. Follow the tarmac footpath into some trees before meeting the main road in the village. (2 miles)

THE SWAN HOTEL STANDS OPPOSITE THE CHURCH IN KINETON

Take time to wander around the spacious village of Butlers Marston. You pass the old manor house and the 15th-century church with its lofty narrow tower. The nave roof is 17th-century; other features to look out for are a tiny peephole, the panelled Jacobean pulpit, and a small triptych showing Our Lord talking with the elders, the entombment, and the stoning of Stephen.

④ Cross over the road and go along **Bank Close** opposite. At its end, turn left up **Bank View** and continue along a signed footpath to the left of the row of cottages. This leads onto a farm track which bends to the right, taking you in a generally north-westerly direction. Go down the track past the sewage works and continue along a footpath by a small plantation of birch trees. Continue along the footpath, with a stream at the bottom of the field to your right. As you progress, the path bends first left and then right to join a good farm track. Head right along the nice track for about half a mile until it eventually bends right to reach the drive to **Oxhouse Farm**, which is to the right. Go left along the drive for the next 500 yards then go right over a stile and cross over the **River Dene** at a footbridge.

Go over the next field and a couple of stiles, crossing a dismantled railway to arrive near a small lake belonging to **Fossdene**

Manor. Bear right along the diverted path walking to the left of the house (between it and the tennis court); then continue along the farm track to the left of the field hedge. The track bends gently right and crosses to the right of the hedge. Continue into the village of **Combrook** to be greeted by lovely Cotswold stone cottages. (2¹/₂ miles)

Combrook has a delightful setting in a deep hollow. There are thatched cottages and the old Norman church of St Mary and St Margaret to admire.

After passing through a farm gate, walk to the right of New Enclosure Farm to arrive at a bend in the road in the village. (2³/₄ miles)

⑤ Head right along the main road into the village, passing to the left of the impressive **church of St Mary and St Margaret**. Walk north along the no-through road towards an attractive row of thatched cottages. Opposite **Chestnut House** go left onto a signed bridlepath by the side of the cottages and to a small gate over a stream; then ascend and bear right into **Knightley Coppice**. Walk alongside **Compton Pools**, where fishermen appear to battle with ducks for fish, and then leave **Knightley Coppice** through a kissing gate and cross the parkland, aiming to the right of the detached houses by **Park Farm**. Continue along the farm drive to the **B4086**; go left and walk along the grass verge for some 200 yards

At the sign for the crossroads with the **B4455**, cross the road and go right, passing through the lodge gates to **Compton Verney** estate. Cross the cattle grid and continue up the estate drive, arcing right past **Home Farm** before entering fields through a farm gate. Go to a second farm gate and then continue, bearing left and descending gently across two more fields; behind you is a good view of the bridge over **Compton Pools**.

Compton Verney is an imposing 18th-century building of grey stone. It was designed by Robert Adam in the Italian style. Inside, it houses a collection of southern and northern European art, an east Asian collection, a British collection, and a rare collection of British folk art, which were brought together by Sir Peter Moores in 1993 with the intention of presenting art in accessible ways.

The 40 acres of parkland in which the mansion stands were laid out by Capability Brown, and include a graceful bridge that crosses over the upper lake. Until the 18th century the church was situated at the edge of the lake near to the house but it was replaced by one nearer to the main house.

Go through a gate in the bottom corner of the second field and then continue up an estate road to cross the **Lighthorne road**. Continue up the road for about 600 yards until you reach the layby at **Lighthorne Rough** woodland. (2¹/₄ miles)

Date walk completed:

BURTON DASSETT COUNTRY PARK WALK

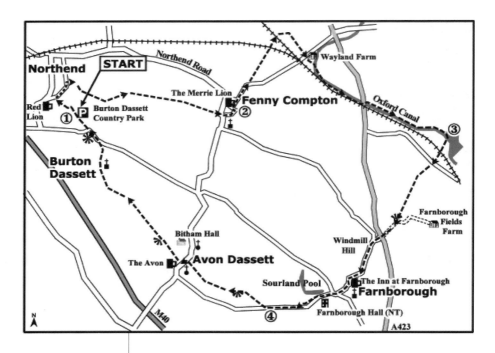

Distance:
10¼ miles

Starting Point:
Burton Dassett
Country Park car
park; there is a
small charge.
GR 394523

Map: OS Explorer 206 Edge Hill and Fenny Compton

How to get there: *Burton Dassett Country Park is
situated 12½ miles south-east of Warwick. It is best
approached from the M40; leave the motorway at junction
12 and go south-west on the B4451. In about three
quarters of a mile go left onto the B4100 and follow the
signs to the country park.*

VIEWS FROM THE HILLS AT BURTON DASSETT COUNTRY PARK

*T*his exhilarating hill walk starts from the beacon at the top of the Burton Dassett Country Park. From here there are magnificent views embracing the Malvern Hills (40 miles), Clee Hills (52 miles), Bredon Hill (28 miles), Meon Hill (14 miles) and Brailes Hill (10 miles). The route takes you into the pretty village of Northend and then across country into Fenny Compton village and from there to the Oxford Canal. Superb Cotswold stone cottages greet you as you enter the main street in Farnborough and you can pause for refreshments at the Vine Inn before visiting 17th-century Farnborough Hall (NT). Finally the route returns to the hills, passing through the lovely Dassett villages on the way.

The Inn, a lovely 16th-century building, was formerly the village butcher's house, and was once called the Butchers Arms. For many years it has been a regular refreshment place for walkers, who enjoy sitting in its delightful gardens. Hook Norton Best, London Pride and Bass real ales are on tap during opening hours, which during the week are from 11 am to 3 pm and from 6 pm to 11 pm. It is open all day on Saturday from 11 am, and on Sunday you are able to get drinks between 12 noon and 10.30 pm.

The landlords are rightly proud of the superb food on offer (between 11 am and 3 pm during the week and all day on Saturday and Sunday). The menu offers a wide range, from filled ciabatta rolls and British cheese ploughman's to fillet steak. The inn specialises in fish and shellfish, and there can be few better places to eat. This is a popular place and Sunday booking is essential. Children are welcome throughout the premises, but dogs are restricted to the bar and the garden. Larger groups of walkers are also welcome, for which discounts can be negotiated; please ring to arrange. Email: office@innatfarnborough.co.uk; telephone: 01295 690615; fax: 01295 690032.

 *The Walk*

① From the beacon go down the footpath to the right of **Bonfire Hill** into the village of **Northend** to arrive in **Hampden Court**. Go right along the main street into **Meldrum Court** in the village.

As you approach the end of the road, go right through a pair of kissing gates and walk the clear footpath going generally eastwards towards **Fenny Compton**. You will walk over a mixture of pastureland and cultivated fields and cross several stiles to arrive in **Grant Close** in the village. Go ahead into **Church Street**, passing the lovely church. (2¹/₂ miles)

Fenny Compton is an attractive village set among the Dassett Hills. The church of St Peter and St Clare stands proudly above the village and is one of only two churches in England with this dedication. The first rector there was a half-brother of Henry III. In the graveyard you can read about Elizabeth Croke, who has lain there since 1719, `a dutiful child, careful to please and fearful to offend; of a modest, mild and merciful temper; pure and unspoiled from the world, she never had an enemy, lived beloved, and died lamented'.

② Bear left, then right, and continue past the **Merrie Lion** pub into the

High Street and **Station Road** (the **Wormleighton** road). At the right-hand bend in the road, go left over a stile onto a path at the back of houses and go half-right (north-east) on the well used footpath. Cross the lane to the Severn Trent works and continue, going beneath the mainline railway line bridge and following the clear path over a cultivated field.

The path bends right and you cross over the **Wormleighton road** before going down to the towpath of the **Oxford Canal** by a mooring area lined with colourful narrowboats.

The 77-mile canal runs from Hawksbury Junction (near Coventry) to Oxford, where it joins the Thames. It is now considered as two sections – the northern and southern – with the connecting three miles now regarded as part of the Grand Union route. A split bridge (which is crossed on the walk) allowed horse-drawn barges to progress without the need to unhitch the horses.

After passing the small marina, walk to the right of the canal and below the railway line. Cross canal

THE INN, FARNBOROUGH

bridge 137 and then go beneath the **A423** road bridge, following the towpath, now on the left bank of the canal. The canal narrows where there was once a tunnel and then widens again; gradually it diverges from the railway line. (2½ miles)

③ At **bridge 139**, go over the canal and continue half-right on a clear track/path. Cross the mainline railway and continue over pastureland, maintaining your south-westerly direction over a series of fields. In about 550 yards you will see **Farnborough Fields Farm** to your far left and the path will soon converge with its driveway. Go along the driveway to the **A423**, which you cross to pick up the road into **Farnborough**. Walk along the main road through the village, passing **the Inn** (set back behind a wall to the left) and the village church before arriving near to **Farnborough Hall** at the end of the village.

The charming village of Farnborough has some beautiful stone and thatched cottages and an old inn that has long been a regular haunt of walkers. The 12th-century church of St Botolph contains memorials to the Raleigh and Holbech families, who, as lords of the manor, resided at the hall for many centuries.

Farnborough Hall is a National Trust property, set amid delightful gardens. The Holbech family acquired the Farnborough estate in 1684, and the superb two-storey, honey-coloured stone house was built soon after. Farnborough Hall and its landscaped gardens have undergone little alteration in the last 200 years and they remain very much as William Holbech left them. The house boasts a wonderful terrace that leads past an Ionic temple and an oval pavilion, which has two storeys and rich plasterwork. There is an obelisk at the end of the 'edge' (hill), and from here there are magnificent views towards Edgehill, Stratford and the Malvern Hills.

At the road junction, head right along the road to **Avon Dassett**, passing the entrance to the hall and continuing past **Sourland Pool**. You can avoid the road for a while by walking along the footpath just inside the trees, returning to the road at the end of the woodland to continue along its side for about 450 yards. (2½ miles)

④ Go right over a stile and cross a cultivated field, pausing from time to time to enjoy the fine view back towards **Farnborough Hall** and the line of the obelisk terrace. A second cultivated field leads into pleasant pastureland with yellow gorse adding a splash of colour in spring. There is a good view to your left as you follow the footpath that hugs the top of the hill over three more fields. The path then descends to the left of a large farm building and emerges on the right of the church in **Avon Dassett**. Go left past the church and walk along the main road in the village for about 75 yards.

The village of Avon Dassett, sometimes called Little Dassett or Dassett Parva, is situated on the slopes of Shooters Hill.

The bells of St John the Baptist church are presently not in use because the church is allegedly moving down the hill. The old church at Avon Dassett had two bells in an enclosed weather-boarded turret over the west end of the nave. The turret had a pyramid roof and weathercock. Being 'unsound and unfit for public worship', the old church was demolished in 1868, and in the same year the foundation stone of the present church was erected on the same site. Bellringers did comment that movement in the tower made ringing difficult at times, and surveys completed in January 2002 by a steeplejack and structural engineer recommend that the bells should not be rung unless the tower were repaired. A recess in the rebuilt church contains a 13th-century coffin with an unusual carving of a deacon.

Just before reaching the **Avon Inn**, go right up a track into open countryside; here you will see the impressive building of **Bitham Hall** up to your right. Continue on the path, which soon hugs the top of fields, until you arrive in the tiny village of **Burton Dassett**, with its lovely Norman church.

Burton Dassett's 13th-century All Saints' church is one of the most beautiful and unspoiled village churches in Warwickshire and has an air of antiquity one rarely experiences. The poet T.S. Eliot wrote in Four Quartets about a place where you can be close to God:

> *You are here to verify,*
> *instruct yourself, or inform*
> *   curiosity*
> *or carry report. You are here to*
> *   kneel*
> *where prayer has been valid.*

Continue along the footpath up to the road edging **Burton Dassett Country Park**. Go left along the road to the car park near to the beacon. (2³/₄ miles)

Date walk completed:

ILMINGTON AND MEON HILL

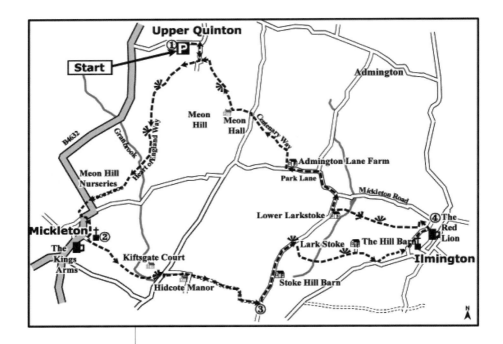

Distance:
10½ miles

Starting Point:
Tailor's Lane in
Upper Quinton.
GR173465. Do
not park on the
village green.

Map: OS Explorer 205 Stratford-upon-Avon and Evesham

How to get there: *Upper Quinton is 7 miles south of
Stratford-upon-Avon. Leave Stratford on the A3400 and
then turn right onto the B4632. In just over 5 miles go left
into Tailor's Lane and park on the grass verge outside the
village of Upper Quinton.*

THE WAR MEMORIAL AT ILMINGTON, WITH THE VILLAGE BEYOND

*T*his is a lovely hill walk encircling historic Meon Hill with its Iron Age hillfort. Beginning in Upper Quinton, it picks up the Heart of England Way, passes through Mickleton and on to Kiftsgate Court, offering the opportunity to visit the National Trust's famous Hidcote Manor Gardens.

The hillfort comprises a double rampart and ditch where a hoard of 394 currency bars were found in the 19th century. Legend says that in the 8th century the Devil sat on Meon Hill and kicked a huge stone towards the recently founded Evesham Abbey. The prayers of the saintly founders of the Abbey upset the Devil's aim and the stone fell on Cleeve Hill, outside Cheltenham, where it was shaped into the base of a cross.

The popular **Red Lion** pub in the village of Ilmington is at the heart of what is arguably the best walking area in Warwickshire, and after a hike up onto the Cotswold hills there is no better way to relax than to tuck into a plate of ham, eggs and chips and to wash them down with a pint of Old Hooky at the Red Lion.

A country pub for most of its 200-year history, it once merely sought to serve the simple but wholesome needs of agricultural workers in the area, and, prior to the Enclosure Acts, the Court Baron met here to discuss who would farm where. Today, very few locals are engaged in the agricultural industry, but the pub has retained its rustic appearance, with stone flags on the floor and small bars. Next door was the old blacksmith's shop in what is now the pub garage. April is a good time to do this walk because if you are here on the right Sunday of the month you will be treated to the Ilmington morris dancers, who can be seen dancing in one of the ten village gardens that are opened for charity.

During the week and on Saturday the pub is open between 11 am and 3 pm and from 6 pm to 11 pm. On Sunday it is open from midday to 10.30 pm. The real ales are Old Hooky and Hooky Best Bitter, and a choice of wholesome pub grub is available.

Well-behaved children and dogs are welcome. Telephone: 01295 263348.

The Walk

① Go to the village green in **Upper Quinton** and bear right, walking southwards towards **Meon Hill**.

In the 1940s a poor homeless old farm labourer was found beneath a pear tree on Meon Hill, stabbed through the chest with the fagging hook which he had been using to lay the hedge. An elderly lady, who declared she was an authority on witchcraft, produced a crop of wild rumours that helped form a local legend, the main elements of which were that the pear tree became an oak; that the sign of a cross had been cut on the victim's chest; and that a phantom black dog had been seen in the vicinity. The case was never solved.

Follow the **Heart of England Way** waymarker bearing right into a field to the right of a cottage; then continue along the footpath that arcs left generally following the contour of **Meon Hill**. Traverse a series of fields and stiles. After about 1 1/4 miles, the path bends to the right, crossing a footbridge and a stile, and then passes between derelict glasshouses to reach the **B4632** in **Mickleton**.

Cross the road with care and go over the stile opposite into pastureland, aiming for a stile positioned in the far left corner of the field. Now head left, walking between shops to reach the **B4632** road near the centre of the village. (You have now entered Gloucestershire.) Go left along the main road for 25 yards; then cross over and go down the lane opposite. Pass through the kissing gate onto a footpath that arcs right by the side of a ha-ha. At the end of the ha-ha, a further kissing gate leads into the **churchyard of St Lawrence**. Go through the churchyard to its small car park. (2¹/₂ miles)

② From the car park head left (south-east) passing through a small gate into a field and go ahead along the **Heart of England Way**. Cross over the field and go through a gate to the left of a hedge and a narrow copse. As you continue you can meander in and out of the trees in the copse, gently arcing right all the while. Where the **Heart of England Way** goes right over a footbridge, continue ahead up a clear path which arcs left as it ascends a delightful short hill called **The Park; Kiftsgate Court** lies to your left. This delightful ascent ends at a gate onto a road, which you cross; then

THE RED LION, ILMINGTON

bear right and then left to go over a field stile. Head up the field and stroll along the edge of **Hidcote Manor Gardens**, which are well worth a visit.

At the top of the rise, go onto the lane leading up to the National Trust property, walking through its large car park onto a good wide track that goes up the hill and passing by some communication masts to reach a country lane. (2¼ miles)

③ Go left along the lane for almost ¾ mile, enjoying the fine view ahead. Turn right over a stile and cross a cultivated field at **Lark Stoke**. A couple of gates will take you to the left of **Upper Lark Stoke Farm** and then you will descend into another lovely dell. After going over a small footbridge (the path may be a little awkward in wet weather), you ascend again to the hilltop, where you join a good farm track that hugs the contour of the hill. There are fine views to your left and soon you will go past the drive to **The Hill Barn** on your left. Go through a farm gate and continue until you approach a road. Do not go onto the road but bear left to go over a stile onto a footpath now going half right (north-easterly) towards the delightful village of **Ilmington**.

The Cotswold village of Ilmington displays a number of the blessings of villages of old. Although it has lost its smithy and bakery, it still has a general store, a post office, a school, and even a hurdle maker. As a result the village has been able to retain much of its appeal for the lucky residents. Two public houses – the Red Lion and the Howard Arms – have survived, and these are very popular with walkers in the area. The entire village offers a dream setting in which to wander and lose oneself in time.

The path will take you to a gate where you enter a hedged track that leads down to **Hurdlers Lane**; taking you to the left of M.D. Vincent's, the hurdle makers, to arrive at **Back Lane** in the village. Head left along **Back Street**, past the church. (The **Red Lion** is in **Front Street**, in the centre of the village). (3 miles)

④ Shortly after passing Ilmington primary school, turn left and stroll up a waymarked, hedged footpath going generally west and maintain this direction as you cross over several fields and stiles, pausing from time to time to enjoy the excellent view to your right. The path crosses from one side of the hedge to the other as you descend into the valley. As you go to the top of the next rise, there is another fine view, with a superb farmhouse at **Lower Lark Stoke**, immediately in front of you. Go down to a pair of stiles near a small pool and walk by the fence on your left to emerge by the gates of the farmhouse and arrive at a tarmac lane, which you now follow. At the road junction go left along **Park Lane** and stroll along this quiet country lane for just over $^1/_2$ mile.

Just after the entrance to **Admington Lane Farm**, go right over a stile onto the **Centenary Way**. Follow the **Centenary Way** in a generally north-westerly direction. The route takes you over a footbridge and through a small gate before crossing a field to reach a stile into a lane by **Homeleigh Cottage**. Turn right along the lane for about 50 yards, and then go left up the driveway towards **Meon Hall**.

In about 350 yards, just before reaching the hall, go right over stiles and across parkland; there is a fine view of **Meon Hill** up to your left. As you reach the brow of the hill, a superb view of the area unfolds, with **Upper Quinton** in the foreground. At the end of the field go through a hand gate and then bear right to a double stile. Now go left and walk to the left of the hedge at the top of the field, passing over a further stile to diagonally cross to a stile on the edge of **Upper Quinton**. Walk to the right of some trees and then go left over a couple of stiles, passing between houses to reach the village road. ($2^3/_4$ miles)

Date walk completed:

BRAILES HILL WALK

THE 13TH-CENTURY CHURCH OF ST THOMAS À BECKET, SUTTON UNDER BRAILES

Distance:
10¼ miles

Map: OS Explorer 191 Banbury, Bicester, and Chipping Norton

Starting Point:
*Park with
consideration by
the roadside near
to Whichford
Wood.
GR 295343*

How to get there: *Whichford is 23 miles south of
Warwick and is best approached from the A3400
Birmingham to Oxford road. Just before reaching Long
Compton, turn left and follow the signposts to Whichford.*

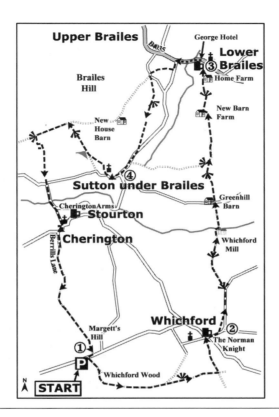

*T*his lovely hill walk with stunning views of Warwickshire takes you through several attractive Cotswold villages. The route begins through a bluebell wood, and then passes lovely Cotswold cottages in Whichford village. Good farm tracks cross a stream by the former Whichford Mill, and then the path climbs above Sutton under Brailes village to open up a vista across to St George's church in Lower Brailes. From here the route descends into Lower Brailes for some well earned refreshment and then on to the picturesque village of Sutton under Brailes to see its delightful village green. Another hill ascent leads to a superb view over the surrounding countryside before the descent into Cherington, and more fine hilly scenery can be enjoyed as you make your way back to Whichford Wood.

All walkers are welcome at the **George Hotel**, which is a regular watering hole for rambling groups in the area. Excellent beer is a major attraction. This is the only Hook Norton pub with six functioning handpumps in one bar and its own page on Hook Norton's website. The Grade II listed building, which, it is claimed, has been serving ale since 1248, boasts stone flagged floors, low ceilings with beams, roaring open fires and 'masses of memorabilia to give it a specially warm welcoming atmosphere'. The George celebrates its Englishness. Like St George's church opposite, it is named after England's patron saint and every year on 23rd April, morris dancers, mummers, musicians and local residents celebrate with a church service followed by entertainment at the George, with beers at the special price of a guinea (£1.05) a pint. The George is open every day from Monday to Saturday, from 11 am to 11 pm, and on Sundays from noon to 10.30 pm. On tap are Hook Norton's Mild, Best Bitter, Old Hooky, VI Generation and seasonal beers. The George is also renowned for good food, which is available throughout opening hours and can be eaten in the lounge or in the extensive gardens. Email: georgehotel@speed-e-mail.com; telephone: 01608 685223.

 *The Walk*

① From the lane by **Whichford Wood**, take the wide woodland track going south-east into the trees. At a junction of tracks bear right and continue up the track until you reach the end of the woodland. Head left into the trees on the track set just inside the edge of the wood. After about ¹/₂ mile, the path arcs right outside the trees – this is delightful woodland walking (especially in spring when the bluebells are in flower). Soon the path curves back into the trees but you continue ahead, following the farm track into open countryside with a view over the village of **Whichford** to your left.

In about ¹/₂ mile, go sharp left and down a good track by the field hedge to arrive on the main street near to the village green. Go right past the **Norman Knight pub**, taking time to enjoy the attractive houses and gardens. (2 miles)

② After passing the last house on the left, head left through a farm gate and take the clear well-walked footpath that cuts off the field corner to reach a second farm gate onto a country lane. Go left up the lane for about 350 yards; then go left again onto a good stone farm drive signed '**North Leasow**' for the next mile. This is superb Cotswold walking; so take your time and enjoy the pleasing views all around. The track drops to go over a small stream by the old **Whichford Mill** and you then ascend again, crossing a lane by **Greenhill Barn**. Your climb continues on a field path over a couple of fields and then levels off.

About ³/₄ mile beyond the mill, look out for and join the track that comes in from the left, from the village of **Sutton under Brailes**, and soon curves left, passing to the right of trees. Bear left through the farm gateway and continue northwards along the waymarked route towards **Lower Brailes**. You will go over a footbridge and some stiles and then ascend a hedged/fenced pathway to emerge on the **B4035** at the side of the **George Hotel**. (2³/₄ miles)

In medieval times, Brailes was the third largest town in Warwickshire; today it comprises a pair of attractive villages tucked away in this area of fertile farmland. Local walkers delight in Brailes Hill, which is the second highest point in Warwickshire. Upper Brailes has old, stone thatched cottages and an earthwork from long ago while Lower Brailes has the superb 14th-century St George's church (known as the Cathedral of the Feldon)

THE GEORGE HOTEL, LOWER BRAILES

with its splendid tower. In a monument above a black marble tomb Richard Davies, the Elizabethan scholar, is remembered with these touching lines:

> *'Though dead he be yet lives his fame,*
> *Like rose in June so smells his name;*
> *Rejoice we at his change, not faint;*
> *Death killed a man but made a saint.'*

③ Head left along the pavement of the **B4035** road towards **Shipston-on-Stour**, taking time to enjoy the attractive village. In about ¹/₄ mile, go left down **Sutton Lane**. When opposite **Jeffs Close**, go right over a field stile and take the clearly signed footpath that hugs the edge of a field until you reach a stile and **Henbrook Lane**. Go left to a hedged bridleway. Do not walk up the bridleway but go ahead over a stile into open countryside and walk for three quarters of a mile along a lovely footpath that descends gently into the valley, crossing over a series of farm fields and stiles. Pause from time to time to enjoy the views. Shortly after passing near to **New House Farm** you will arrive on **Sutton Lane** once again. Head right along the lane and into the delightful village of **Sutton under Brailes**. (2 miles)

It is like stepping back in time to visit lovely Sutton under Brailes, for it maintains one of the best village greens I have ever come across, and its lovely 13th-century church is peacefully set away from the road among old tombs and a fine spreading chestnut tree.

④ After passing the lovely village green, which is surrounded by very attractive houses, you will reach the church. Go right up the clear path to the left of the church building and diagonally cross the field at its rear, then crossing a stile onto a farm track. Head right up this good track and you will pass to the right of some trees and a pond. Continue up the track, going over a stile as you climb up the hill, but do pause from time to time to recover your breath and to enjoy a very pleasant view over **Sutton under Brailes** behind you.

As you approach the brow of the hill you will reach a bridlegate on your right. Here, go left, away from the gate, and follow a path going half left (south-west). Pass through a couple of farm gates as you descend gently to a final farm gate and you will soon enjoy a superb view that embraces **Burmington**, **Willington**, and **Shipston-on-Stour**. At the gate, go left, following the waymarker signs through a kissing gate and then curve right past some old buildings. The path then bends left and descends, becoming part of a wide, hedged track. After passing some more farm buildings, go through a farm gate to a lane, then continue climbing to reach the corner of the next lane. Continue ahead, bearing right by **Cherington Mill** (the **Cherington Arms** pub is along the road to the left) to enter **Cherington** village.

Quaint is the word to describe Cherington, where thatched cottages are common. Despite the fact that the Cherington Arms pub sign shows a buxom lady with an armful of fruit, the village's name has absolutely nothing to do with cherries. It most probably means 'village with a church', and its lovely church has a 15th-century tower overlooking the valley. Look out for the sculptures of long-eared men and strange beasts with human arms which appear under the roof beams of the church.

After passing by the church, you will reach the main road in the village. Go right for a few yards and then go left up **Berrills Lane**. The lane soon becomes a track that takes you back into lovely open countryside to start a stretch that continues for about $^3/_4$ mile. Follow the direction of the clear waymarkers as you walk in a generally southerly direction. Soon you will be ascending past **Margett's Hill Coppice** to reach a gate onto a lane with the car park to the right. (3$^1/_2$ miles)

Date walk completed:

LONG COMPTON AND THE ROLLRIGHT STONES

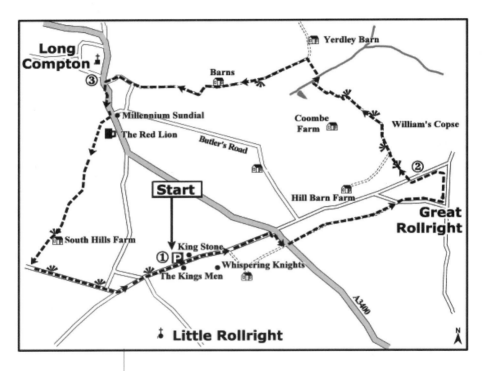

Distance:
7¼ miles

Starting Point:
The small car park next to the Rollright Stones.
GR 296309

Map: OS Explorer 191 Banbury, Bicester, and Chipping Norton

How to get there: *The Rollright Stones are situated some 25 miles south of Warwick and are best approached from the A3400 (Birmingham to Oxford road) at Long Compton. Just after passing through the village of Long Compton, turn right up the lane signed to Little Rollright. Bear left at the top of the lane to reach the Rollright Stones.*

LYCH-GATE TO THE CHURCH OF ST PETER AND ST PAUL IN LONG COMPTON

*T*his is a pleasant hill walk that starts by the famous Rollright Stones and passes into attractive Cotswold countryside. A delightful woodland path used by the local residents of Great Rollright offers superb views over the village of Long Compton, as you commence a pleasing descent into the village. In this area are some of the best hills in Warwickshire; so take your time to enjoy the fine views and to experience the history of the villages, where thatched cottages appear to be on every corner. The fine church of St George in Long Compton is a landmark in the area, and its unusual lych-gate will catch your eye. After pausing for refreshments at the Red Lion there is another testing hill ascent to return to the mysterious stones.

A fine 18th-century hotel, the **Red Lion** offers old world charm, with open fires and cosy corners. The long bar has a warm, inviting atmosphere with its roaring log fire, exposed stonewalls, and low oak beams. An interesting collection of bottled beers and agricultural implements, together with paintings by local artists, is on display, and the friendly atmosphere is enjoyed by locals and visitors alike. Walkers are particularly welcome, and the locals like you to join in the banter. Above the fire you will find the delicious menu specials listed and between 12 noon and 2 pm each day you may select traditional pub food from the menu or from the daily specials board to eat in the bar, the lounge, or the lovely garden. On a summer's day there is no better place to enjoy a meal than the large country garden. In the evening you may wish to visit the charming restaurant area, which is decorated in cottage style with prints, maps, and brasses, a warm glow coming through from the lounge area. Here you can relax in an intimate atmosphere and enjoy a splendid candlelit dinner. Wherever you eat you will appreciate the no-smoking policy. For a quick evening meal, visit on Tuesday for curry night or Wednesday for fish and chips, to eat in or take away!

During the week and on Saturday the hotel is open from 11 am to 2.30 pm and from 6 pm to 11 pm, and on Sunday from 12 noon to 3 pm and 7 pm to 10.30 pm. Hook Norton Best bitter and Websters Yorkshire Bitter are the named real ales on tap with a guest beer to complement. Enjoy the hospitality with the excellent choice of beers, wines and spirits. After a super country walk in the glorious Cotswolds the Red Lion Hotel is the ideal place to refresh body and spirit. Website: www.theredlion.cotswoldinns.com; email:redlionhot@aol.com; telephone: 01608 684221.

On a windswept hill above the village of Long Compton can be found the awe-inspiring Rollright Stones. This great circle of 60 monoliths was erected many years before the Romans came to Britain and is much older than Stonehenge. Today, the stones spread across the county border, with the 'King Stone', which stands 9 ft high, in Warwickshire, while across the road in neighbouring Oxfordshire is the main group of monoliths of which the highest stone is a little over 7 ft tall and the smallest 4 ft. Four hundred yards away is a further group of stones called 'The Whispering Knights'.

There are many legends related to the stones and numerous stories as to how they arrived. The most endearing legend tells how a king proposed to invade and conquer England but was stopped by a witch as he ascended the hill from Great Rollright. She told him to take seven strides and said,

'If Long Compton thou canst see
King of England thou shalt be.'

He marched forward with his men thinking this to be easy. However, after the seventh stride Long Compton disappeared out of sight behind a mound of earth. The witch said to him:

'As Long Compton thou canst
not see

King of England thou shalt not be.
Rise up stick and stand still,
stone,
For King of England thou shalt
be none.
Thou and thy men hoarstones
shalt be,
And I shall be an eldern tree.'

Thus the witch turned the king into a standing stone (the 9ft King Stone) and his men became the monoliths on the other side of the road.

THE RED LION HOTEL, LONG COMPTON

The Walk

① After you have visited the stones, go along the lane in a north-easterly direction (left from the **King Stone**). Just before reaching the busy **A3400** road, turn right up some steps and walk around the left edge of the cultivated field (the **A3400** is over the hedge) to arrive at a farm track coming in from the right. Turn left, go over the **A3400**, and then climb the bank opposite. Now walk along the excellent farm track that runs parallel with a minor road. In about ³/₄ mile you will reach the minor road and here you have a choice: either go right and head up the quiet road towards **Great Rollright** village or enter the trees opposite and stroll along the very attractive, well walked local path that runs parallel with the road. Just before reaching the road junction in the village, go left and continue along a good bridleway by the trees. At the end of the field, the track becomes a footpath and bends left; continue by the side of the field hedge and in about 350 yards, go right through a gap in the hedge to a quiet lane. (2¹/₂ miles)

② Cross the lane, go through the farm gate opposite and follow the waymark direction to reach another farm gate in the far right-hand corner of the cultivated field, pausing to enjoy a very fine view ahead over the village of **Long Compton**. Bear right onto the farm track, which then bends left to go through a further farm gate. The track now hugs the right-hand hedge of the next field as you continue your descent, still enjoying the view. The track curves right until you reach trees on the edge of **William's Copse**. Here you go through a hand gate and continue your descent to the right of the field hedge, following a line of posts which mark the edge of the farm track. At the bottom of the field the route bends right and then left to negotiate a footbridge over a stream before climbing gently to another farm track with **Yardley Barn** in the trees up to your right.

Go left along the track, passing through a farm gate with a delightful hill away to your right. After passing a collection of large barns, the track goes left and then right, and soon you will arrive on the outskirts of **Long Compton**. Stroll along **Vicarage Lane** up to the main **Shipston road** through the village. (2¹/₄ miles)

A delight of stone and thatched cottages and an intriguing lychgate add to the charm of Long Compton, which is situated in some of the loveliest countryside in Warwickshire. Picturesque cottages appear to line the busy A3400 road through the village.

The 13th-century church of St Peter and St Paul is near to the road and in the battlements of the church building are loopholes which may have been used by marksmen in the Civil War. But it is the quaint lychgate which catches the eye; it is in fact a two-storey thatched cottage, built mainly of stone with bits of wattle and daub and with somewhat crazy little windows. It is believed that originally it may have been a priest's house, and in more recent times it has been the village cobbler's shop. The lower storey has since been removed, and this is now the main entrance to the churchyard.

③ Head left up the pavement, past the fascinating Millennium sundial to reach the **Red Lion Hotel**. Retrace your steps into the main village for about 50 yards; then, immediately after a private house, go left through farm gates onto a clear path, walking now in a generally south-westerly direction. After going through the second gate, the path climbs gently, following the half-right (south-westerly) line over the next two fields and two stiles to arrive at a third stile by farm buildings. Here, go left and then right onto a farm track to pass the farm buildings. As the track arcs left continue ahead over a cultivated field aiming for a stile in its top left-hand corner. Maintain your direction and continue heading towards **South Hills Farm**, passing through a couple of farm gates. A fine view of **Long Compton** is emerging behind you; so spare time to enjoy this and catch your breath. The route takes you to the right of **South Hills Farm** and you cross a final field to reach a stone stile onto a road by a junction of tracks and roads.

Go left along the road for about $1/2$ mile until you reach a road junction; there is a lovely view to the left over **Long Compton** and towards **Brailes**. At the road junction, continue ahead and you will soon reach the **Rollright Stones** again. ($2^1/_2$ miles)

Date walk completed: